HOW TO ...

support children with Autism Spectrum Condition in primary school

Lynn McCann

Acknowledgements

I would like to thank all the SENCOs, teaching staff and parents that I have worked with over the past ten years, in special education, primary and secondary schools. You have all taught me so much, you have worked so hard and together we've seen so many children and young people overcome challenges and thrive in school.

To the children who are autistic, thank you. You are talented, interesting, unique and a joy to work with. I hope this book helps your teachers support you well and that you go on to be the best person that you could ever be.

To my husband Steve and my children Siobhan and Matthew, I love you, and thank you for putting up with my constant autism chatter.

How to support children with Autism Spectrum Condition in primary school

ISBN: 978-1-85503-599-7

© Lynn McCann 2016
Illustrations by Robin Lawrie

This edition published 2016
10 9 8 7 6 5 4

Printed in the UK by Page Bros (Norwich) Ltd
Designed and typeset by Andy Wilson for Green Desert Ltd

LDA, 2 Gregory Street, Hyde, Cheshire, SK14 4HR

www.ldalearning.com

CONTENTS

CD-ROM contents
Social communication checklist
Classroom environment audit
Work time visual support
Home–school communication template
Problem solving map
Sensory monitoring sheet
Behaviour support plan
Group Activity – structuring social stories
STAR record
Pupil passport template
Social skills board

All websites were correct at the time of going to print.

PREFACE

My career began in a mainstream primary school where I soon became a Special Educational Needs Co-ordinator (SENCO), which I loved. I spent a short time as a Childhood Studies lecturer and then moved to a specialist school for children with Autism Spectrum Condition (ASC). Whilst I was there, I had the chance to set up an outreach service to support local mainstream schools with children with ASC. This was the perfect way to combine my mainstream and special education school experience.

I now lead a team of independent autism consultants, working with children from Early Years through to KS4, and continue to develop support, advice, training and resources which help to make school successful for children with ASC. This book shares my knowledge and experience with classroom teachers and staff who want to support children with ASC with the right strategies for them personally.

This book is for SENCOs, teachers, teaching assistants and senior managers. It is intended to be used as a reference throughout the time a child with ASC is in your school or class. It will help you understand the child's condition and support their strengths and differences. The schools I have worked with have always appreciated practical and adaptable resources, and some of the resources I have developed over the years are in a photocopiable format on the CD-ROM so that you can adapt them and use them with the children in your school. I hope you find them helpful.

Every child with ASC is individual and the key is to understand them and *their* autism, because the way it 'works' in each child is unique.

Learning and discovering together is part of the joy of the ASC journey. Let the child be your guide as you build a relationship of trust and learn how to communicate with each other.

Please note that while every effort has been made to use inclusive language, the term 'parent' has been used for the sake of brevity in many cases, but can also refer to a young person's carer.

CHAPTER 1
What is ASC?

The term Autism Spectrum Condition (ASC) has had a number of labels over the years. It encompasses the labels *Asperger syndrome* and *autism*. Many professionals and authorities use the term Autism Spectrum Disorder (ASD), but more and more professionals (like the eminent autism researcher Simon Baron-Cohen) are adopting the term 'condition' rather than 'disorder'. Autism is a difference in the way the brain processes experiences, information and sensory stimulation, and there are often strengths and talents associated with this. Therefore, it seems proper that we see it as a 'condition' rather than a 'disorder'. This is important as around 700,000 people in the UK are on the autism spectrum (National Autistic Society, 2012). Some people with ASC have associated learning disabilities and co-morbid conditions, nonetheless with the right support many are able to achieve academically and in life as the general population.

'Children with ASC' or 'autistic children'?
There is a lot of debate amongst the autism community and within professional circles about whether to use person-first or identity-first terms for someone who is on the autism spectrum. Some adults may prefer the term 'autistic' as it defines who they are. However, many professionals continue to use person-first language. This book uses the term 'children with ASC', but recognises the preference that some may have to be spoken of as 'autistic'. It is recommended that any SENCO or teacher asks the pupil and their parents to identify which term they prefer.

ASC is a condition that a person is born with and will have all their lives. It is generally accepted that it is a difference in the way the brain is 'wired' and is part of human neurodiversity. A person with ASC can have difficulties or differences in communicating and understanding communication with people around them, socialising and understanding the complexity of social information. They may have strong and sometimes rigid thinking patterns, find guessing what others might think difficult and have differences in the way their senses experience the world. They may also have strong emotional responses and differences in the way they process emotions.

ASC, by definition, makes every person with ASC unique and the way it impacts on them will present a unique set of strengths and challenges in this lifelong condition.

Diagnosis

Every child with autism is different but will share certain characteristics in various degrees if they are to receive a diagnosis. Currently, two sets of criteria are used in the UK for the diagnosis of ASC. These are contained in the International Statistical Classification of Diseases manual (ICD-10®, 2016) and the American Diagnostic and Statistical Manual of Mental Disorders (DSM-5®, 2013). These documents identify the characteristics of autism as being marked differences and impairments in social communication and interaction, with restricted interests and rigid and repetitive behaviours. The DSM-5® now includes the area of sensory processing, which is an important change.

Some parents may be keen to seek a diagnosis, some may be reluctant and others may not want to have any label for their child and so refuse to seek a diagnosis. All parents have the right to seek or refuse to seek a diagnosis. A class teacher should not approach a parent and say they think their child has autism. If they think that a child has 'autistic tendencies' concerns should be raised through the school SEND channels and parents informed of the particular difficulties their child has, rather than anyone using the term 'autism'. These should be recorded and documented along with the strengths of the child and strategies that support them. It can be suggested that the parent visits their GP or Health Visitor, or that the school has the child assessed by an Educational Psychologist. The NICE Guidelines (2011) suggest that there should be an **Autism Pathway** set up in each area so that a full and comprehensive assessment can be made that includes detailed interviews with parents and the child; details of child's experiences at home, school and other settings; their medical and developmental history and consideration given to other conditions that may be affecting the child. Ideally this should involve a multi-disciplinary team involving a paediatrician, speech and language therapist (SALT), clinical or educational psychologist and having access to advice and reports from other professionals such as an occupational therapist and specialist nurse. They usually go through a recognised assessment process such as the Autism Diagnostic Observation Schedule (ADOS).

Unfortunately, the realities of current budget cuts mean that in some areas only one professional is responsible for diagnosing ASC and parents must check that this person is fully qualified autism professional.

This process takes some time if done correctly. Parents can wait for at least 6-8 months once they have been referred for diagnosis whilst all the evidence is collected and team meetings are convened to discuss the findings. The support given to the child can begin and develop whether there is a diagnosis or not. Good support always is about knowing the child's strengths and weaknesses.

Once a family is given a diagnosis they will go through many emotions and will take time to come to terms with it. They will want the best for their child but may also be bombarded with information and suggested strategies, or given no follow up support at all. As teachers, you will need to be aware of these emotions and difficulties so that you can build a supportive relationship with parents as they travel through this process. This book may help everybody involved learn about what will be the best support for the child.

Too often focus is placed on their difficulties instead of their strengths and children become labeled disruptive or unable to achieve. This is not true. All children with ASC are capable of making progress and achieving success if the right understanding, support and expectations are in place for them by parents working together with teachers and teaching assistants (TAs) that they meet each year in school.

Looking at the world from an autistic viewpoint

To help teaching staff understand how ASC affects how children experience everything in their lives, it is valuable to look at the following areas in more detail through the perspective of children with ASC and consider the stresses and demands that they may experience every day.

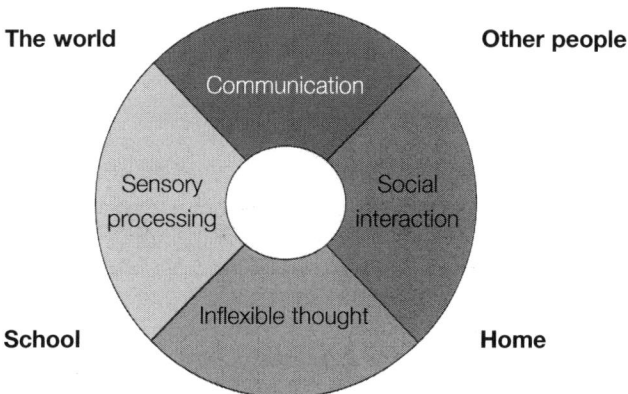

Communication

The communication skills of children with ASC vary widely. Many children with ASC will have had (or still have) delayed language development as a young child and may have received speech therapy in the Early Years and possibly throughout primary school. Others will have had (or still have) almost precocious speech with complex vocabulary and the ability to memorise large chunks of dialogue. However, what is common in all children with ASC is their difficulty in understanding and processing spoken language, and creating spoken language quick enough to meet the demands of the situation.

> Children with ASC often understand language literally. Therefore, everything that is said to them is understood without taking into account any inference, implied meaning, context or sarcasm. For these children, figures of speech such as metaphors and idioms can be very confusing.

Being able to read non-verbal communication may be difficult for these children and impact on their understanding of the words being spoken. In school, the ability to turn what they know into coherent written communication can be very difficult for some, especially if it is imaginative, abstract, requires them to explain different opinions or is something in which they have no interest.

Not understanding how we use inference and tone of voice to emphasise meaning can result in children with ASC missing and misunderstanding a lot of the communication in class and around school.

Social interaction

Every situation throughout a child's day demands communication with others, including interactions with their family in the morning, travelling to and walking into school, trying to find familiar people amongst a lot of unfamiliar faces in the playground, different classrooms and teachers, sudden changes of personnel, break times and lunchtimes, and finally home time. This may also be followed by a trip to the shop or going out with their parents. As ASC affects children's social development, they may have limited skills in socially interacting with different groups of people.

Generally, children develop social skills through some instruction but also through an enormous capacity to assimilate what they see others doing into their own behaviour. A lot of this development happens naturally for children, but children with ASC often have very uneven social development across a number of issues, which are discussed below:

Eye contact

Some children with ASC have difficulty using eye contact which means that they miss the connection with other people that shows shared attention, trust and non-verbal communication. Some may even have **face-blindness** (i.e. the inability to recognise even familiar faces) which means recognising even their close family and classmates may be difficult. Others may use their peripheral vision to limit the intense overload their brain receives from looking directly at a person or situation. They are then able to see what is around them without the pain and discomfort caused by looking at something directly. Sometimes this can result in them being accused of not paying attention.

Non-verbal communication

It is common in children with ASC to have little ability to 'read' a person's non-verbal communication. Facial expressions, body language, gestures and posture can all seem threatening and confusing or, for some, make no sense at all.

Hypersensitivity

Some children with ASC are hypersensitive to non-verbal communication. They see every detail in facial expressions, body language and sense all the emotion in those around them and find all of it, all at once, difficult to process. They can be easily overwhelmed, may seem anxious, withdrawn or unable to communicate effectively, maybe cautious about going to places where there are many people and very anxious when around others, particularly when in small or large groups. Sometimes this can cause meltdowns or shutdowns when their brain cannot deal with the enormity of emotion and stress.

Conversation

Understanding the social conventions and rules of conversation may be difficult to grasp for children with ASC. Some may cope by dominating conversation, insisting on talking about their special interest every time, or seem to interrupt all the time. Others may be withdrawn or very quiet and feel anxious when a contribution to a conversation is demanded of them.

Difficulties making and keeping friends

The complexities of friendships may be quite overwhelming for children with ASC and they may easily become left without friends or vulnerable to teasing and bullying. They want friends who have the same interests as them and will make them feel comfortable. Loyalty is very important as they may not have the skills to repair communication breakdowns.

Inflexible thought

Research using MRI brain scans shows us that the autistic brain may be 'wired' differently to a neurotypical brain. This can mean that certain skills are more efficient in the autistic brain, such as seeing patterns, systemising, being an expert in one area of interest, and visual processing. Whereas, other skills can be much less efficiently processed in the autistic brain, such as social communication and understanding, predicting social outcomes, planning, self-organising, self-monitoring, emotional communication and imagining what a hypothetical situation might be like (Wertz, 2012). These skills are related to the part of the brain which deals with **executive functioning**. Executive functioning refers to the thinking skills that help the brain organise and act on information. These skills enable children to plan, organise, remember things, prioritise, self-monitor, pay attention and know how to start activities. Being able to use information and experiences from the past to solve current problems is also an executive function. These skills are often limited in children with ASC (even into adulthood) and this can have a number of effects on children in daily life. These include:

Anxiety about change

Difficulty in predicting what something will be like can mean a child with ASC is resistant to and very anxious about change. Sometimes even small changes (such as not using their usual pen or sitting in a different place) can cause extreme anxiety. Often changes in school are not communicated well to children and so a substitute teacher, a timetable change, the child's TA being seconded to another activity and other changes can cause extreme anxiety, withdrawal or meltdowns.

Self-organisation

Many children with ASC find it difficult to organise themselves, which impacts on their ability to do things like get ready for a lesson, tidy up, get changed for PE and gather all the things they need for home time. Poor executive functioning can also affect their ability to start a piece of work independently; the brain cannot move on to the work without some kind of prompt or support to get started. In some children with ASC, this is quite severe and a lot of support is needed for every piece of work.

Understanding points of view

A common difficulty for children with ASC is understanding different points of view and perspectives on a situation which differ to their own. This rigidity of thinking can cause them difficulties in accessing the curriculum, getting along with others and interpreting incidents that happen around school. They may also become fixated on an issue or event that they feel very strongly about, finding it difficult to move on from or stop thinking about it.

Memory and recall

Some children with ASC find it difficult to organise and recall things in their memory. They may be able to recall lots of facts and information about their own interests but unable to recall what they did in a lesson yesterday. This may be linked to a poor concept of time because we store events in time order in our memory. For a child with ASC, thinking of where to find the information in their jumbled memory can take too long to process in the time they have.

Motivation and self-esteem

Children with ASC may show poor motivation when faced with subjects and activities they are not interested in, don't understand or think they may fail at. Some pupils may refuse to do the work perhaps because they have had some difficulty with a task or subject in the past. They may feel so anxious that refusing to do the work seems more logical than trying to do it.

Children with ASC often form an intense fascination with a special interest, their understanding and expert knowledge of their field of interest brings feelings of pleasure and success. Their special interests can be used as a link to build their self-esteem and success in areas they may not find easy. For example, a pupil who was intensely interested in plumbing systems was given a task to do with the caretaker to support his maths and writing, and later went on to be an apprentice plumber.

Sensory processing

Sensory processing is the brain's ability to organise and regulate the aspects of the sensory system. All the information we take in from the world around us comes in through our senses and dictates how we respond to changes in our own body and the environment, as well as how we interact or respond to the situations and people we come into contact with.

Sensory processing disorder (SPD) is a condition where a person struggles to effectively process multi-sensory information from the senses. Having a SPD makes it difficult for a child to filter their senses or 'switch off' from sensory overload, impacting on their daily experiences at home, school and out in the community. Some may find that they get great pleasure out of certain sensory experiences (e.g. spinning, jumping or twisting something) and will crave the joy that engaging in these experiences might bring them. Others may seek out smells or tastes or want to touch everything. Conversely, some children with SPD experience heightened sensations and find the world far too loud, smelly and overwhelming, leading to anxiety and distress.

When identifying a child's needs it is important to consider if they experience sensory difficulties as it will have an impact on their ability to access social interaction and learning.

Strengths of ASC

Having an autistic brain may have certain strengths and advantages. Common strengths include:

➤ **Observing things in fine detail.** The ability to see fine detail and remember things that seem unimportant to others can support artistic or musical ability, mathematical knowledge, scientific or other subject expertise and excellent report writing.

➤ **Logical reasoning.** Thinking about a problem logically can be a very useful strength in all areas of the curriculum and in life. When others may be blinded by emotional responses, a child with autism may be able to state a logical and truthful observation or answer. It is possible to harness this in the classroom and support the child with ASC to bring their logical reasoning to a group problem-solving activity. It is important to listen to them and make them feel that their contribution is valuable but also teach them that others may have different ideas and opinions and that it is okay for them to do so.

➤ **Adherence to rules.** This can mean that the child is eager to get things right and complete a task to fulfil the rules. However, this may lead to some considerable anxiety which will require support.

- **Honesty and loyalty**. This can result in lifelong friendships. Honesty may sometimes not be what others want to hear but we can support this by teaching others to appreciate it and not take things too personally. Supporting friendships in the early days will be important so that they can grow and become established.

- **Visual thinking**. If visual strategies are used for those who are visual thinkers, then their ability to think about a task and learn can be greatly enhanced. However, it is important to check each child's learning strengths and not assume that all children with ASC are visual learners.

- **Computer skills**. Many children with ASC are very gifted in using computers and their skills should be channelled into supporting their school work appropriately.

- **Sense of humour**. There are a number of comedians with ASC (e.g. Dan Aykroyd). Getting to know a child's sense of humour can be one of the most rewarding ways of interacting with them.

Like any other child, children with ASC have their own personality and life experiences and should be encouraged to bring out the best of their talents and skills. Developing their area of expertise and giving them the opportunity to coach and support others can encourage them to take a caring role and develop their empathy.

Some children with ASC (especially high-functioning children in KS2) can also be great advocates for ASC awareness and support within schools. They can talk about their condition to help others understand and promote tolerance and inclusion.

Girls with ASC

Up until very recently it was believed that there were far more boys than girls with ASC and it is still the case that many more boys are diagnosed than girls. However, recent research shows that there are far more girls on the autism spectrum than previously thought. This is due in part to the assumption that girls are less likely to have ASC than boys, and also to ASC presenting differently in girls compared with boys, resulting in many girls on the autism spectrum being misdiagnosed or remaining undiagnosed (Gould & Ashton-Smith, 2011). If you think a girl in your class may be on the autism spectrum, then seek advice from an autism specialist teacher or an educational psychologist, who will be able to guide you and her parents through the process of diagnosis. Some of the features to look out for in girls are listed below.

Communication

Boys with ASC are often identified by their behaviour. When they cannot find the words to use, they use actions either to make their needs known or in reaction to distressing situations. Whilst girls with ASC can also do this, they are often more passive. They may internalise their distress and be more vulnerable to mental health issues. They may be withdrawn or moody or just ignore the demands made of them, rather than challenge them.

Girls with ASC may speak in a babyish tone or have no regard for the hierarchy of authority in school, so they can be seen as cheeky or rude when they are just stating facts. Girls, like boys, often take language literally and so misunderstanding and confusion prevents them really appreciating what is going on around them or what a teacher really means. Conversely, they can also be extremely articulate and able in certain subjects.

A girl with ASC may use coping mechanisms by imitating the social behaviours of those around her. However, she may not be able to discriminate which behaviours are appropriate and which are not. This can make her extremely vulnerable to social isolation or to doing anything that others suggest, just to fit in.

Social interaction

Girls on the autism spectrum can seem more socially active than the boys but they can want to dominate and be in control of the friendship group, or cope by imitating the social behaviour of a group. Often they cannot cope with jokes, teasing and communication breakdowns. They may be moody, withdraw or throw a tantrum when things are difficult for them. On the other hand, they may seem the life and soul of a group but struggle to maintain the friendships beyond a basic level.

Girls on the autism spectrum can 'feel' intensely. They may experience intense shame when they don't get something right, especially socially. They often cannot tell the difference between a small social mistake (something that others would just brush off and move on from) or a big social mistake that marks someone out as odd. Consequently, they can feel a lot of stress and awkwardness when they are in any classroom group or social situation.

Inflexible thought

To an onlooker, the play of girls with ASC can seem very imaginative and they appear to lose themselves intensely in books and characters. However, on closer inspection their play is very strict and controlled (e.g. a doll is called a name, given a character and nothing can change that identity once it has been assigned).

The special interests of girls with ASC can be seemingly usual interests for girls, such as ponies or princesses, but they can become very intense and all-consuming. Childhood interests can continue into the later primary years of Y5 and Y6, when their peers are moving on to pre-adolescent interests. This is often a diagnostic characteristic for girls with ASC.

Girls with ASC can have the same difficulties with lack of organisation and planning as boys on the spectrum do. On the contrary, they may be obsessive organisers who need to control everything to avoid becoming very distressed. Change and new situations will be difficult and girls can be as likely as boys to exhibit characteristics of Pathological Demand Avoidance (PDA).

Sensory processing

Dealing with a busy, noisy, smelly, confusing world can be the most stressful thing that a girl with ASC has to deal with. She may be experiencing the world intensively due to a SPD and need support to identify sensory seeking or avoiding behaviours. The best course of action may be to have a sensory assessment done by a specialist occupational therapist (OT) who can then provide a programme of sensory therapy.

The issues that cause difficulty for girls with ASC can be more evident in KS2 as social complexities and relationships around them develop rapidly and can leave them behind. Dealing with friendships, gossip, teasing, emotional awareness, social media and self-image can expose girls with ASC more than boys. This is due to the nature of the relationships girls and boys usually develop in these years. Both boys and girls with ASC may find themselves excluded from parties, bullied and vulnerable to depression, so it is important to be aware that girls with ASC need extra support in school too.

Conditions co-morbid to ASC

It is not uncommon for children with ASC to be diagnosed with additional conditions. Sometimes ADHD, dyslexia, Developmental Co-ordination Disorder (DCD) – formerly known as dyspraxia, PDA, Obsessive Compulsive Disorder (OCD), Tourette syndrome or other conditions may have been recorded as part of a multi-diagnosis. It is important in these situations that staff know about these other conditions and build strategies that are recommended to support them into their approach along with the ASC support strategies. Often, these strategies will complement each other and can work well alongside the usual classroom practice if they are planned and used consistently.

Pathological Demand Avoidance

PDA is increasingly recognised as part of the autism spectrum by clinicians, and therefore more children are being given a diagnosis of PDA along with their ASC. However, it remains a controversial condition, and isn't part of the official diagnostic manual (DSM-5) or recognised by all clinicians. PDA is characterised by extreme anxiety and manipulation to avoid everyday demands. It is almost like having a panic attack whenever the person perceives there may be a demand upon them. This can include the everyday demands of getting out of bed and getting ready for school, someone saying their name and getting through the routines of the day. This high anxiety leaves the individual in a constant state of 'fight or flight' and extra demands, such as those given by a teacher in order to do a piece of work, or by a parent to do a small task such as pick up their socks, can bring on a panic attack. Some individuals may seem to be in a constant state of meltdown and exhibit challenging behaviours in order to avoid doing the activity demanded of them; others may cope by micro-managing their lives in rituals, routines and manipulating others to try and minimalise their anxiety. Children who are suspected of having PDA are often more socially-able than children with ASC and need a lot of specialised support to enable them to cope with their fear of demands at home and school.

If you have a child with a diagnosis of PDA, you will need to consider the strategies that you use with caution. Some of the strategies suggested in this book will work well with children with PDA and some will not. For example, demands with choices that give them some control over what they do work well, whereas a visual timetable where the demands of the whole day are presented in one go tends to increase anxiety. The PDA Society website is a good resource for PDA-specific strategies, which generally include much more flexible choices and negotiation than those suggested for a child with ASC but not PDA.

What to do if you suspect a child may have ASC

It is inevitable that teaching staff will suspect that a child may have ASC at some point in their career. It may be that concerns are brought to you by parents and you may or may not have already noticed those issues in your classroom. As you notice differences between a child and their peers, such as unusual behaviours or difficulties in coping with school, it is important not to rush into labelling the child as having 'autistic tendencies' or indeed, autism.

Seeking a diagnosis will need parental consent and a referral to a multi-disciplinary assessment team, either through Child and Adolescent Mental Health Services (CAMHS) or a specific autism assessment team if this is available in your area. You can find out what is available in your area by contacting your NHS Clinical Commissioner. Parents can seek a referral through their GP, health visitor, speech and language therapist (SALT) or paediatrician, but the professional they are referred to needs to be trained in autism diagnosis. An observation and questionnaire-based test called an

Autism Diagnostic Observation Schedule (ADOS) is usually used to collect information from the different settings the child spends time in. This should include information requested from school. Schools can request a SEN assessment which will often involve an assessment by an educational psychologist. If the parents approach the NHS it is more likely to include a clinical psychologist, sometimes a speech and language therapist and/or paediatrician doctor.

The SENCO will be the point of contact at the school and any concerns the parent or teacher have should be referred to the SENCO. The school should begin to collect evidence, using the SEND Code of Practice (2015) cycle of Assess, Plan, Do, Review. Any diagnostic pathway should seek information from the school about the child's strengths, differences and difficulties.

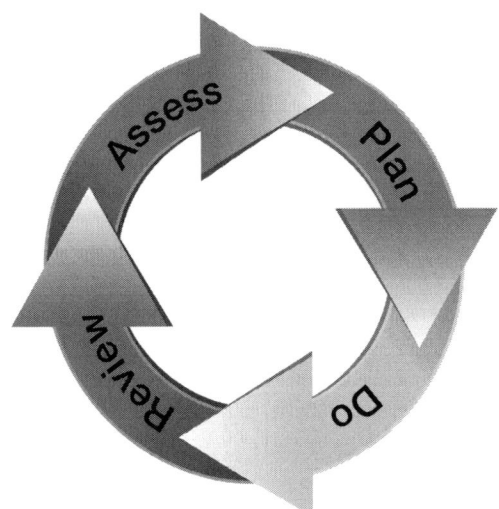

The strategies in this book are generally based on good communication, structure and support that can benefit any child, and can therefore be implemented as part of the Assess, Plan, Do, Review cycle. The Early Years Autism Observation Profile for Early Years or non-verbal children (Cumine, Dunlop & Stevenson, 2009) and/or the **social communication checklist for KS1–2 children on the CD-ROM** can be used at the assessment stage along with any academic profiles a school might use. The school should write the strategies into a child's Individual Support Plan so that the implementation, effectiveness and progress of the strategies can be monitored. This can form the basis of evidence for diagnosis and for an application for an Education, Health and Care (EHC) Plan assessment if the school and parents wish to pursue this.

CHAPTER 2
The environment

The classroom is each teacher's mini-kingdom and the 'home' of their pupils for most of the school day. Teachers lavish care and attention on how it is set out and how they decorate it, and spend time organising furniture and equipment that they and their pupils will need to access throughout the year. In primary classrooms, hours are spent printing and laminating and setting out displays, and carefully choosing words, pictures and prompts for writing, maths and topic work. Coat pegs and drawers are labelled, boxes and books are given out and groups of tables are given a name. In the Early Years, parts of the room are often sectioned off into creative, 'small world' or sensory play areas and most classrooms have a common focus area, usually in front of the whiteboard, where children will gather to listen to the teacher presenting a lesson. At the beginning of the school year, the classroom is bright, stimulating, labelled, and ready for a new intake of children.

Now imagine you are standing in a busy foreign railway station. You know you have to get somewhere but you're not quite sure how to read the strange symbols that indicate the destination on your ticket. The signs are in a script that you don't recognise, the trains are loud, noisy and smell strongly of diesel. The buzzing crowd is pushing and jostling you in a direction you're not even sure you want to go. Some people come towards you making attempts to grab your bag, and you feel scared and threatened. Some people gesticulate with signs and mouth strange words, but you don't understand and they soon go away. You spot what looks like an official and make your way to them, but they  are just shouting random words in a language you don't understand through a megaphone. Your head hurts, you are sick with anxiety and frustration and you have no idea how to cope.

School can feel like this for children with Autism Spectrum Condition (ASC).

Sensory processing overload can be the first difficulty for children with ASC as soon as they find themselves in a noisy, stimulating environment with a moving crowd of people they don't know, and whose gestures, language and intentions they can't read. Language processing difficulties can lead to much of what is being communicated to them passing them by. They can feel as if people are trying to give them things or take things away from them randomly. When things keep changing, or as they are moved from one activity to another, their inflexibility of thought means they can find it hard to switch attention. Social interaction difficulties make others around them seem unpredictable and confusing, and they often invade their space or make demands they cannot understand. All the while they are trying desperately to shut out the distractions, noise, smells, movements and activity that come in a constant stream of demand as a result of sensory processing overload. They can get cross and frustrated because as soon as they engage in something they actually like, an adult attempts to move them onto something else.

This is often more acute in the earlier years of primary school, but there are children with ASC who find school this stressful throughout KS2 as well. The first thing teachers can do if they have a child with ASC in their class is to lower the arousal of the classroom environment so that the child has a calmer and more navigable space in which to become more independent.

Early Years Foundation Stage – Nursery and Reception

The Early Years classroom is a play-based and sensory environment. It promotes exploration and investigation, and many types of play and social skills through choice, sharing, co-operation and scaffolded activity.

Stimulating environments are popular in Early Years classrooms. Walls are usually highly decorated, there are lots of activities and types of equipment available at all times and there are often displays hanging from the ceilings, low enough to be seen by very small children.

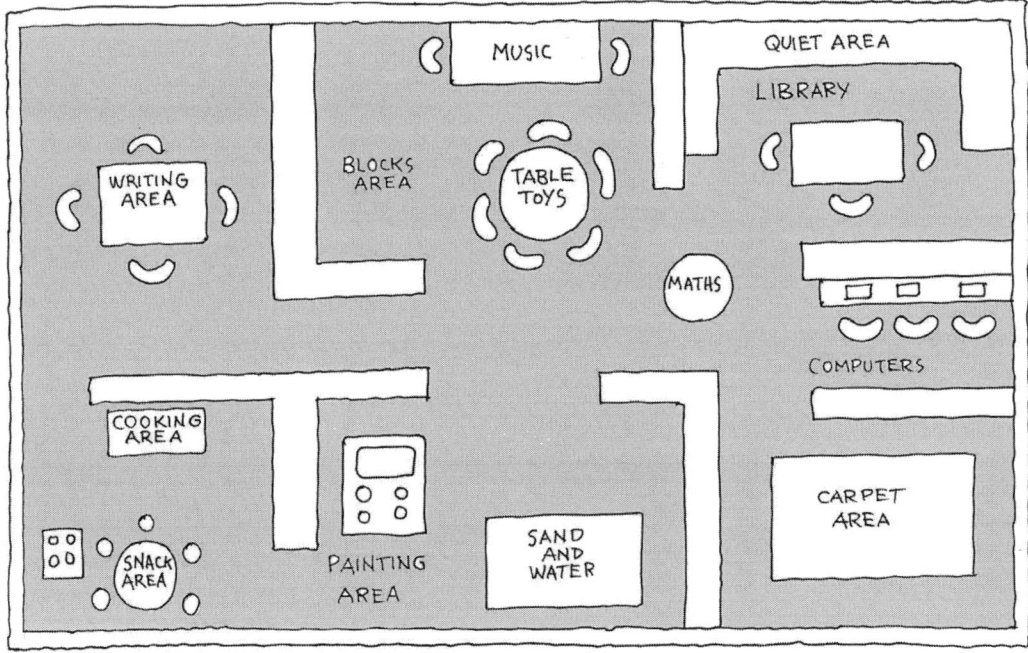

This plan shows a typical Reception classroom. It is tightly packed and you can imagine that when it is full of children, moving about might be difficult. An Early Years classroom can be adapted to be more ASC-friendly. This can be done by carefully planning the area to help all children move around smoothly, access information and do activities more independently, and give visual direction that can support communication and language skills. The aim should be to reduce sensory overload and give all children the best environment in which to learn. An assessment of the environment can be carried out using the **classroom environment audit on the CD-ROM**.

Case study

Gemma (Reception pupil) was finding the classroom overwhelming and this showed in the way she would often stand in the middle of the room covering her ears and crying. If staff tried to engage her in an activity she would only do what they prompted her to do and then wait for them to do the next thing, without showing any motivation to try things for herself. The teachers decided to rearrange the room, having less out at once and leaving some clear space between activities. They also reduced the amount of display on the walls, took down the things hanging from the ceiling that weren't part of an activity and made a quiet corner with a dark tent and sensory toys. Gemma began to enjoy the sensory area first and then began to explore the other areas one by one. The calmer classroom enabled her to take the time she needed to adjust to each area and the sensory area became her refuge when she became anxious.

Top tips for creating an ASC-friendly Early Years classroom

1 Consider doing a risk assessment of the inside and outside environments from the child's point of view.

2 Lighting can be a real issue for some children who are sight-sensitive. Strip lighting can be overwhelming as they see every flicker (almost like strobe lighting), and natural light from windows (regardless of size) can mean they function differently on bright days because they cannot see as well. If possible, it is a good idea to change fluorescent lights to light sources that do not flicker and have blinds on windows so that light levels can be controlled.

3 Make enough space to enable children to move around each table or area easily. Think about how the space works when the whole class is in it and see if you can make movement flow easier. Get down to their level and work out how you would plan to get from one activity to another as safely as possible.

4 Use plain table coverings. Patterns can make visual processing more difficult and a child may not be able to focus on the equipment or activity if the pattern on the tablecloth is overwhelming.

5 Think about creating displays that stay within a border and try to use straight borders rather than wavy ones. Try to use plain-coloured lettering for displays rather than patterned letters and keep a space between each element of the display. Try not to cover every bit of wall and plan some calm spaces (i.e. plain, pale-coloured walls) between displays.

6 Have one-topic displays (e.g. one display for letters and phonics, one display for numbers). Try to keep things hanging from the ceiling to a minimum and keep them to one area of the classroom only. This will allow children with ASC to see across the room and move around it more independently because they can plan their route.

7 If you want children to focus on the whiteboard during carpet time, then have display-free walls around the whiteboard. If there are a lot of posters and displays around it, children

with ASC may not know what to focus on, or be very distracted by them. Some children may need a carpet square so that they know where their place is on the floor. Alternatively, you could stick a grid on the carpet with masking tape so that each child has their own space which is not touching another child.

8   All labels on boxes and equipment for childrens' use should have pictures or photographs on as well as words. This supports all pupils' developing independence, but especially for those pupils who have language difficulties.

9   Place photos or visual schedules at each table to enable all children to have a clearer idea of the instructions and possibilities of the activity. These can include how to put on an apron, how many pupils can play there and where to put finished pieces such as models or paintings. (See Chapter 4 for more about visual communication.)

10 Consider making a low-arousal sensory area where children, especially those with ASC, can 'escape' to in order to avoid sensory overload or extreme frustration from constant language and interaction demands. This can be a simple pop-up tent or screened-off area. It could have soft cushions and beanbags, fabric to cuddle or hide under, headphones and a small box of the child's favourite construction or sensory calming toys. (See Chapter 6 for more about supporting sensory processing.) Show the child with ASC that they can use this area when they feel overwhelmed or need a quieter place to work or play for a while.

11 Outside areas can be very attractive to children with ASC as they enjoy the increased freedom and different activities they bring. (Remember that for some children with ASC outside areas will be more overwhelming). Some of the principles above will also apply to outside spaces to help a child with ASC manage this part of the Early Years environment (e.g. space to move around, calming as well as stimulating walls, clear visual supports). Most outdoor areas are very secure, but additional support may be needed to assess the risk of children absconding into other areas or out of school.

Key Stage 1 – Y1 and Y2

In these years, primary school pupils make the transition from a play-based curriculum to curriculum based on listening, sitting, writing and language. Although there will still be practical activities, the purpose of these becomes more directed and children are expected to sit at tables and engage in writing-based activity for increasingly lengthy periods of time. Outside time becomes timetabled rather than available as they choose. If they haven't been before, children are introduced to regular lessons of phonics and PE, and assemblies and playtimes with the rest of the school. Y1 and Y2 classrooms tend to become more structured and orderly, and there is less moving around. This environment can suit some children with ASC better than the Reception classroom, whereas others will find the transition and increased demands to sit and listen quite a challenge.

Case study

Simon (Y2 pupil) was invited by his teacher to dedicate one display board in the classroom to his special interest subject, which was electronics. He was allowed to keep the display all year and was thrilled when other children began to give him things to put on it. This greatly supported his friendships as children were often seen talking to Simon about his interest.

Top tips for creating an ASC-friendly KS1 classroom

1 Use different colours for groups of tables or chairs so that children can distinguish one from another easily. If children are asked to move places, then give children with ASC a name card to put on the chair they want to sit on if they get anxious about the change. (See Chapter 6 for more about supporting sensory processing.)

2 Put the equipment needed for an activity in a 'table tidy' such as a compartmental tray so that it is easily accessible and means a child with ASC (and their peers) do not need to wander or become inactive because they haven't got the right equipment.

3 Used different colours for exercise books for different subjects and make the key visually available to pupils.

4 Use a class visual timetable to support all children. (See Chapter 4 for more about visual communication.)

5 Make sure there are clear, labelled (with photos works well) places to put things like finished work, models and artwork.

6 Differentiate displays with different colours, with space between them and straight borders. The lettering on them should be plain and they should display only one topic.

7 Avoid things hanging from the ceiling and displays and posters around the whiteboard.

8 Keep the classroom tidy so that there are not things in the way (visually or physically) and things are not difficult to find.

9 Walk through the fire alarm routine with children with ASC and take pictures or write a list of the routine to follow. Try to warn them of any impending fire alarm practice if you know that noise or change will really upset them.

Key Stage 2 – Y3, Y4, Y5 and Y6

Often, KS2 children with ASC have become more accustomed to the school environment and can be less sensitive to changes, sensory issues and noise. Others are just as sensitive to the environment as they have always been. Catering for individual needs can be a challenge but by this stage, a child's needs and support should be well-known and documented so that one teacher can pass on what strategies work to the next. If a child is new to the school in KS2, then an assessment of their needs will need to be done, including their reactions and sensitivities to the environment.

Sensory overload in the school environment is the most common reason for a child's mainstream placement breaking down. This is because it leads to extreme anxiety, which can lead to disruptive or challenging behaviours as the child struggles to cope with and communicate their difficulties. Solutions could be something as simple as the teacher using non-perfumed deodorant, or toning down the displays and clutter in the classroom. Other children with ASC may need a detailed sensory programme that addresses a wider range of issues with environmental adaptations that work together to make school more accessible for the child. Children with sensory overload will need support, and the children themselves need to learn to recognise their own needs and understand how to regulate those needs so they can understand what options are available to them.

Case study

Beth (Y4 pupil) was becoming increasingly anxious as there was so much going on in her environment. She refused to line up or get changed for PE and if she was told she had to, she would nip, kick or push other children. She complained loudly, screamed if something changed and was very unhappy.

Beth's teachers discovered that she was over-sensitive to touch and spent most of each day in fear that someone would brush past, touch or bump into her. She was given a seat with a soft fleecy cover on it, had a spare chair next to her at the table and whenever the class had to line up, she was allowed to stand at the end of the line. She was allowed to wear soft jogging pants for PE and get changed in a separate area. As a result of these strategies, Beth settled down and found school much more bearable.

Top tips for creating an ASC-friendly KS2 classroom

1 Group tables are common in KS2. It is a good aim to have a child with ASC working alongside others on a group table, but if they cannot cope with this then consider where the best place for them to sit might be. There may be a place in the classroom where there are minimal distractions which will help the pupil access learning. Make sure they can see the whiteboard without having to look over other children's heads. Involve the child in this decision wherever possible.

2 If the child has a teaching assistant (TA) working with them, try not to isolate them by sitting the TA between them and other children. TAs should be working towards the child's social inclusion and independence, so make the TA chair a temporary stopping place for when the child needs their help and ensure the child has good role models and children with shared interests to work alongside the rest of the time.

3 Equipment and books need to be accessible. Children with ASC may need their own things near them, or conversely, put out of reach if they are likely to fiddle too much. As they move through the KS2 years, they need to be able to access and manage equipment more independently. Consider colour-coding, providing visual labels and giving children the responsibility of handing out equipment themselves to support this.

4 Children may need access to their own curriculum support lists on their table or in their book. Don't expect them to easily access words, punctuation, maths help and other support that you have put around the room on your displays.

5 Moving around school and the playground may still be problematic for children with ASC in KS2. Make sure environmental checks are done each year and do not assume that a pupil can automatically deal with any changes that might have happened in the school building or grounds during the holidays. **Use the classroom enviroment audit on the CD-ROM.**

6 New experiences, such as going out of school on trips, will need their own environmental audit. Do not assume children with ASC will know where unfamiliar cloakrooms, toilets and entrances are.

Adapting the classroom environment

It is difficult and unnecessary to completely change the primary classroom environment just for one or two children. However, some important and focused changes can make a lot of difference to children with ASC accessing school and learning. It is important to support them in the same way as any other child with SEND and make adaptations that are reasonable. Generally, reducing sensory stimulation works best alongside having a calm, low-arousal and safe place available for a child to go to if they are stressed and need a break.

Lighting, temperature, space, colour and organisation can have a huge impact on a child's access to learning. Small changes in these can make a massive difference. When schools do not change anything, the result is often that children with ASC struggle to focus on or engage with their learning, their behaviour will reflect their inability to cope and the whole placement can break down.

Case study

Devi (Y3 pupil) attended a tiny rural school where his classroom had to be packed away to be used as a hall each day. Though no fault of the school, this caused great stress for him. He did not cope at all with this total change in his environment and his behaviour became more and more challenging as his stress levels rose. The school had nowhere to let him go to feel calm. Devi's parents eventually changed his school to one where the environment was much better for him and he began to thrive.

As a teacher, it can be nerve-wracking to change your environment. You may feel that the other children will suffer as a result (although there is little evidence of this). However, it can be very effective for children with ASC. If you have the luxury of knowing in advance that a child with ASC is coming into your class, it would be helpful to be mindful of their specific difficulties when planning the room.

CHAPTER 3
Communication support

Autism Spectrum Condition (ASC) is characterised by difficulties in processing language, and both expressive (spoken) and receptive (understanding what is heard) language is affected. However, communication involves much more than language. Being able to interpret the social, non-verbal messages of communication is a large and difficult part of learning to communicate for people with ASC.

Being unable to be an effective communicator and receiver of communication becomes one of the greatest barriers to education, social relationships and life's opportunities for children with ASC.

Communication is a two-way process and involves understanding that we are sending a message to other people and that they are sending messages to us. These messages are only partly the words we use; much of what we communicate is through reading non-verbal messages. This enables us to make reasonably accurate guesses about what the other person may be thinking, as well as judgements about the validity and sincerity of what they are saying.

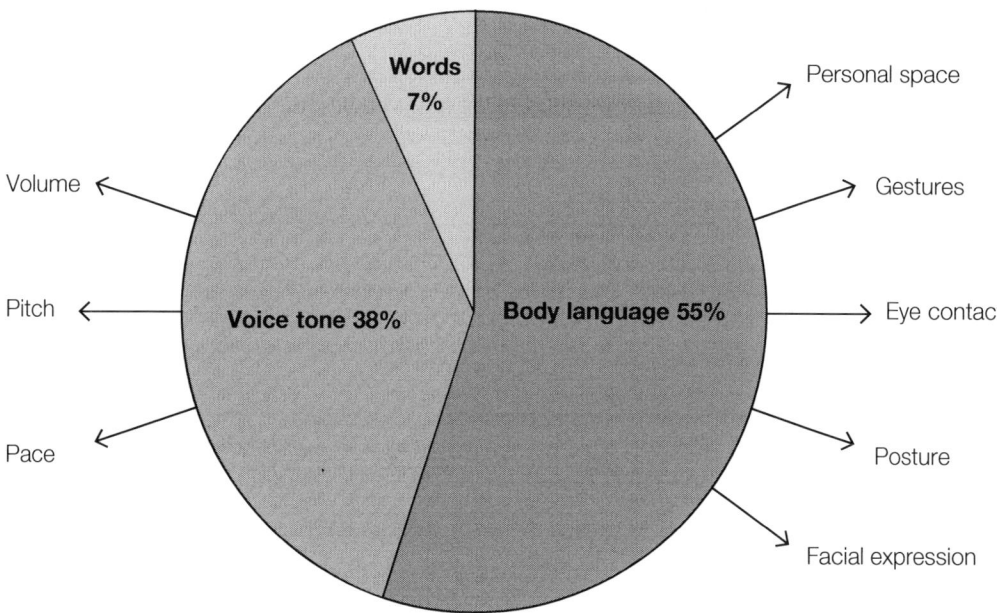

Aspects of communication

The messages that people send to each other need interpreting, and multiple messages sent all at once (such as in a group discussion or conversation) require rapid shifts in attention and multiple interpretations that can often be baffling for children with ASC. Add to this sarcasm, insincerity, lies, jokes and the unspoken 'rules' of conversation (e.g. taking turns, listener awareness, social conventions, politeness, banter, apologies, interrupting), and we have a world of communication that can be very frustrating and confusing for children with ASC.

Children with language delay

Some children with ASC will have delayed language and therefore require a lot of support to help them learn to communicate. They may be able to use some words and gestures but be unable to talk beyond immediate needs, or only by using echolaic words and phrases. Sensory sensitivities may also make it hard for children with ASC to distinguish voice sounds from other sounds in the environment (Ellis et al, 2010).

Children with ASC often have a delay in processing verbal communication and it is possible that whilst the child is trying to make sense of what has been said, the speaker has quickly moved on to the next instruction or piece of information. Articulation difficulties can also be evident in children with ASC, and an understanding of the purpose or social use of speech and vocal communication can take longer to develop.

However, it is wrong to assume that non-verbal children with ASC cannot understand what is being said. Technology has opened up the world of communication for many children who cannot speak, but have much to say. Computers, communication aids and specialist apps are used more and more in schools.

Echolalia

Echolalia (repeating words and phrases) is a feature of communication that occurs in early language development of all children. As a child begins to talk, they repeat sounds, words and phrases without purpose or context. Once a child develops an understanding of language for communicating their use of echolalia decreases and they will use a variety of words and phrases from their memory with purpose. Echolalia can occur for a longer period of time in children with ASC as they may struggle to develop spontaneous language. It is an important part of learning how to use words for children with ASC and should be used to support them in using language more purposefully and as a strategy to support them in situations where they need to speak but find it difficult to know what to say.

Case study

Nathaniel (Reception) rushed around the class saying lines from his favourite *Toy Story* film. This began with him saying these to himself, but he later started to direct his phrases towards adults and other children. He was delighted when they answered him and even more so if they said '*To infinity and beyond!*'.

This amusing game became the foundation of interactions with his peers, and his peers began to seek him out to talk to him. Years later, Nathaniel had learned to say much more first by becoming more sophisticated in his echolalia and then by becoming more able to create his own independent language. This enabled him to develop some good relationships with the other children in his class, being able to chat with them about all kinds of things.

Children without language delay

Other children with ASC have what seem to be typical speech and language skills, and some may have precocious verbal skills at an early age. They may be **hyperlexic** (i.e. able to read very early) and seem to be able to discuss complex topics at length. You may notice, however, that their verbal skills are very much focused on their own interests and particular observations, and that they would often rather talk to adults than their peers.

Children with superior verbal ability are often diagnosed much later than children with language delay as it can be assumed that they have no communication difficulties; their ability to use expressive language can mask the difficulties they have with receptive language. Teachers may notice, however, that a child seems to be struggling to understand inference and metaphors, and/or they may take things literally and their conversation skills with their peers may seem very one-sided or immature. Some children seem to dominate every conversation or constantly interrupt or use inappropriate words, highlighting their communication abilities. These children often need as much support for their social communication and understanding as a child with less verbal language.

Identifying the communication needs of ASC children

Usually a child with speech difficulties will be seen by a speech and language therapist (SALT). However, if they have competent speech and vocabulary they may not be eligible. Every child with ASC will have some communication difficulties, and even very able and verbal children can misunderstand much of the language and communication that goes on around them, impairing their learning and social relationships.

A child with ASC may not achieve their academic potential if they have good verbal ability or factual knowledge but poor ability to apply, organise or record accurately. It can become clear that they are actually missing a significant amount of what is being taught through not being able to keep up with the pace of verbal language and ideas communicated. It is useful for the class teacher to spend some time observing and collecting evidence about how a child with ASC functions during normal classroom routines and lessons. Observe whether they have poor responses to instructions and directions, just follow others, or stand back altogether. Can they organise themselves to start and complete a piece of work? Do they understand the meaning of what is being taught?

Developing communication in the Early Years

The approach for each child with ASC will be based on their individual needs, which should be assessed as soon as possible (preferably by an ASC-specialist SALT). If a child hasn't got a diagnosis of ASC, then their communication and other needs will need a fuller investigation by a SALT.

The Early Years classroom is a communication-rich environment. There are words, letters, stories, songs, texts and learning experiences to encourage language all day, every day. However, this can be overwhelming for a child with ASC and they may not be able to easily assimilate the language they see and hear around them. A child with ASC will need a more focused and directed approach that is tailored to their needs. There are some common principles and approaches that can benefit all children with ASC below:

Developing play and language

Follow a child's lead by playing alongside them and imitating their actions and vocalisations. (Programmes such as Intensive Interaction and Floortime™ promote this approach.) This promotes a relationship of trust with the child and helps them develop the early communication skills of shared attention, interacting with others and sharing their interests, as well as gently introducing opportunities to look at others and imitate each other. Once trust and positive interaction have been established, you can introduce some communication games and songs, and bring other children in to join in with the play. If all the staff are trained in and understand this approach, then the child with ASC can benefit from interacting with different people who are consistent in their approach and understanding.

Giving clear instructions

Be direct and give one instruction at a time. Children with ASC need time to process what you have asked them to do, and the more direct and concrete the instruction is the more they are able to understand it. Don't use a lot of words; only use key words. Consider the two requests below:

The second instruction tells them that the instruction is for them (*Jack*), what it involves (*coat*) and what to do (*on*). It seems very abrupt but it is clear and effective. A child with ASC can take a few seconds to process what you have said and if you rush into saying something else, they won't have had time to process what you said first, resulting in confusion and distress.

Children with ASC benefit from being given one instruction at a time. Use set vocabulary to help them follow a series of instructions:

> 'First, (do this)… [pause] … Next, (do this)… [pause] … Then, (do this)… [pause] … Well done!'

As they become more confident you can use *'First… Next… Then…'* to give two or three-step instructions. Eventually, you can teach the child to organise their own tasks using *'First, I will… Next, I will… Then, I will…'*, which is a good communication and organisation skill for their academic work.

Visual support for communication

What should be used as visual support will depend on the child's conceptual understanding. With very young children, objects of reference (such as a cup to show it is time to have a drink) may be needed. Once children have the ability to understand symbolic representation, photos of objects or places can be used, and then symbols and words. Visual support enables communication with the child about what will happen, what choices are available and what instruction they are being given. (See Chapter 4 for more about visual communication.)

Sign language

For some children who have very little verbal ability, signing systems such as Makaton or Signalong may be helpful. These systems can be used with verbal language and focus on key words in a sentence. Learning signs that everyone can use can help with understanding and be part of the communication support used for a child with ASC. You may need to make sure that the child does respond to using signs when they are first introduced as some may not find it helpful at all.

Picture Exchange Communication System (PECS)

Some children may be introduced to PECS, a communication system originally devised for non-verbal people with ASC based on using cards with pictures to communicate wants and comments. Adults can give a child a card to communicate an instruction, or a child can give an adult or another child a card to communicate their wants and needs. Children are taught to use these cards in six stages:

1 how to communicate – physical exchange
2 traveling and persisting in communicating
3 picture discrimination – choice
4 sentences – structuring requests
5 answering questions – simple sentence answers
6 making comments – extending vocabulary

It is designed so that children's communication can progress to using whole sentences, commenting on activities and events and expressing opinions even when they find verbally expressing these difficult. This approach needs to be introduced and monitored by a specialist teacher or speech and language therapist (SALT), who should also provide training and resources for teaching staff to use with the child.

There are also apps that use the same principle as PECS devised by Frost & Brody (1994), enabling a child to choose a picture or symbol on a tablet rather than having to pick up a card. Schools often buy symbol-based software so they can print off symbols that children will need to communicate in the classroom, at home and in the community. The two most popular packages are Widgit Communicate in Print™ and Boardmaker™. They allow staff to print off simple, consistent and easy-to-interpret symbols for PECS cards, visual timetables and visual symbols. Both packages also have writing-with-symbols functions, which can support a child's writing development.

There are other technology-based resources for communication that are appealing and effective for children with ASC. Some devices allow a child to type in words that are then spoken by the device. Apps on phones and tablets and software that displays symbols with text are also helpful in supporting communication skills for children with ASC. However, much depends on a child's individual needs and it is important to have support from a specialist teacher, educational psychologist or SALT to assess their abilities, understanding and needs before investing in any communication system or software.

Developing communication in KS1

In KS1, children with ASC will need more support with their language and communication skills in order to access the curriculum, which will involve not only following instructions but also making comments and asking and answering questions about different topics, and learning related vocabulary. They may also need support in developing their attention skills so that they can listen and process language for communication and learning.

Children in KS1 are developing their reading and writing skills and beginning to form their own creative communication in words, roleplay and writing. These activities may be difficult for a child with ASC unless the communication and learning experiences are relevant and meaningful for them. Their particular interests should be harnessed to support their development in communication and learning how to successfully interact with others.

Recommendations

- Children with ASC may need help using language for self-organisation, asking for help, calming strategies, responding to verbal directions and joining in.
- Keep language for instructions simple and at a child's level. It is important to get their attention first and model appropriate responses. Pause, wait and repeat as necessary so that they have time to process the language, and give feedback. Both non-verbal and verbal children benefit from being given simple one-step instructions, not being rushed and being given time to process the instruction.
- Social communication can be modelled and supported by teaching children how to greet others, how to ask if they can play with something and respond to others' greetings and attempts to interact.
- It is very helpful to say what you *do* want rather than what you *don't* want (e.g. *'please walk'* is easier for a child with ASC to process than *'don't run'*).
- Avoid assuming that children with ASC know what you mean. Be concrete and literal in what you say. You may need to explain what something means that others will automatically 'get'. (This is especially true for sarcasm and idioms.)

➤ Using the words first, next and then in communication with children with ASC can enable them to learn about ordering and sequencing and help them with memorising information and recalling events.

➤ Consider using the word *finished* instead of *stop*. Often, *stop* results in a temporary cessation of an activity (e.g. 'stop when the bell rings at playtime' might see a child start running again as soon as the bell ceases) whereas the word *finished* communicates that the activity is ending and will not continue.

➤ Use visual communication strategies to support access to learning.

Developing communication in KS2

In mainstream KS2, we can assume that children with ASC have made progress in their use and understanding of communication. They may continue to have speech and language therapy, but this is less common at this stage unless the child has significant speech problems. Even if a child's verbal ability is good, it is important to continually check on their understanding and comprehension of the subtle meanings and inferences of language.

Children with ASC may also continue to need time to process instructions and information and need visual support to enable them to become more independent. In upper KS2, it is important to prepare the child with ASC for the communication challenges of going to secondary school, where they will meet new and different teachers and children, and have new subjects.

Recommendations

➤ Teach aspects of communication such as intonation, speed, paired and group conversation, asking and answering questions, pronouns and body language.

➤ Teach group work skills and practise how to shift attention to others and their ideas. Start with pair work, sharing ideas, co-operating and discussing.

➤ Teach verbal problem-solving skills such as how to ask for clarification, help and time to think, how to be assertive without being aggressive and how to get out of awkward situations.

➤ Teach inference skills for reading comprehension tasks. Ask questions about what is happening, predicting what will happen, what clues there are to tell us what something really means, and about the situation when something isn't stated literally.

➤ Help children with ASC understand idioms, metaphors, jokes and non-literal language through fun and visual activities.

➤ Where possible, give children with ASC opportunities for public speaking (e.g. talking about their favourite subject to an audience, going out into the community and learning how to order food, buy a ticket or introduce themselves) and teach them how to ask for help and how to leave an awkward situation. Role play and practice can help build a child's communication confidence and works best when their parents and school support them together.

➤ Develop a child's social communication confidence and understanding through activities such as those in Chapter 10.

CHAPTER 4
Visual communication

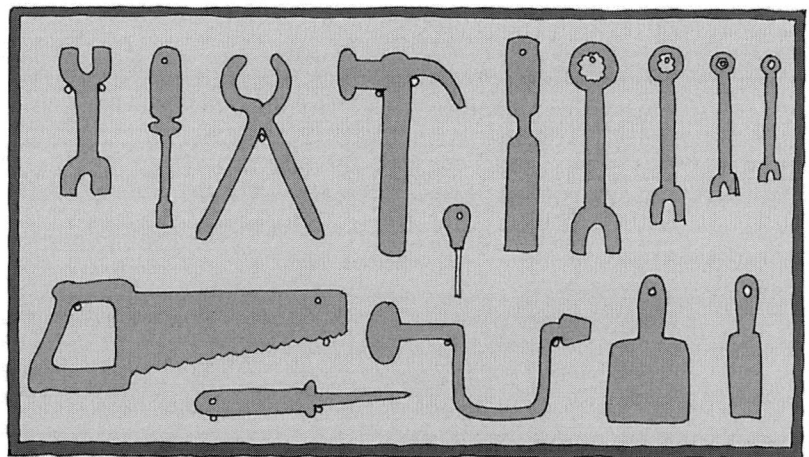

A factory or garage shadow board

Consider the picture above. If you worked in a garage or factory and you needed to put tools away in the right place, then a visual picture or outline of each tool would make it very clear where each one should go. Even if you can't read or speak a particular language, pictures communicate quickly and efficiently.

Research by Roa & Gagie (2006), Hodgdon (2000) and Goodman & Williams (2007) has shown that visual communication helps children with ASC for a number of reasons:

- Many people with ASC report that they often think in pictures and are able to process pictures more easily than verbal language.
- Visuals are available for longer so that children don't have to rely on their memory of what has been communicated whilst trying to process what it is they have to do in order to respond to the communication.
- Visuals help those with little or no speech to communicate their wants and needs.
- Visuals are part of everyone's communication; we write things down, draw maps, send each other pictures. This helps children with ASC to access a common language.
- Visuals can reduce anxiety, enable things to be put in a list or sequence easily, and remind children what will happen next or in the future.

Visual objects, pictures or symbols can be meaningful, accurate and succinct. When used well, they can help children make sense of what is going on in the classroom and gain access to the world. They can help to teach routines and skills, enable independence and encourage positive behaviour, as well as give the child a means of communicating their wants, needs, feelings and ideas. Visuals can support access to the curriculum and help children be successful in recording and writing.

It is important to match the kinds of visual supports used to an individual child with ASC and make sure that they do actually find them helpful. Not all children with ASC will find visuals helpful; this will depend on their age; language level; reading, comprehension and processing ability; and personal preferences. Below are some of the ways that visuals can be used and suggestions for adapting them for different levels of understanding and for progression as children move through school.

Visual timetables

Often the first advice given to teaching staff is to use a visual timetable. This could be a simple First/Next Schedule (see below) or a more complicated breakdown of the school day. It is important to think about how a visual timetable supports a child and how they are going to use it. All too often, visual timetables become 'wallpaper' on the classroom wall and are not really used as they should be to support the child.

If used well, visual timetables will:

- ➤ give information about what will be happening and when.
- ➤ give the day its structure.
- ➤ support transition and coping with changes.
- ➤ teach children how to organise themselves and become independent by following step-by-step visual instructions.
- ➤ support a child's memory, sequencing skills and concept of time.

Visual timetables should be introduced at different developmental stages, as outlined below.

1 First/Next (Now/Then) schedules

A First/Next (or Now/Then) schedule is the first visual timetable that should be introduced to a young child with ASC and may help them transition from one activity to the next. It can be supported by reference objects and is most often introduced for children who are non-verbal and have little understanding of communication.

First/Next schedules work best when most of the activities are those preferred by the child. They can be used alongside a choice board with pictures or symbols of the choices available to the child (if the child is able to make choices about their activities) so that organisation skills are introduced, enabling children to decide what they will do first and next. A choice board can help a child who is easily overwhelmed by too many choices. You would introduce only two choices to begin with and then build up to a wider variety of choices.

2 Pictorial schedules

Move on to an extended schedule when the child is able to so that they can see that a longer period of time will be sectioned into a number of activities. For a young child with ASC, knowing the structure of the whole session can enable them to understand how it will be structured. Photographic or pictorial schedules may be needed at first as the child must be able to 'read' and understand symbolic representation before moving on to symbol-based schedules.

The child should be supported to take off the picture or symbol for each activity as it finishes and post it into a 'Finished' pocket at the bottom of the timetable. This ensures that they know when an activity has ended and teaches them to manage their own timetable and move on to the next activity independently.

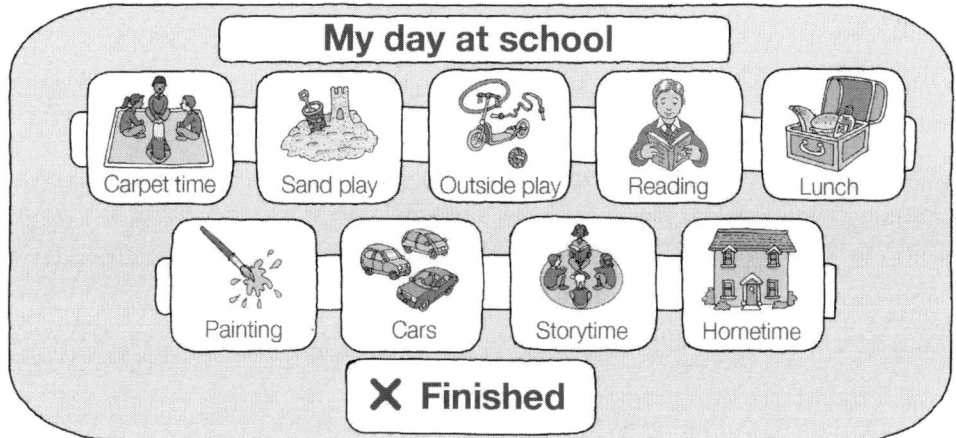

3 Symbol-based timetables

Once the child is able to understand visual symbols and is able to read some words, these can be combined to provide a timetable that they should be able to manage themselves. These can also be class timetables that the whole class uses. Many classes do have class visual timetables and they work best when a 'monitor' (possibly the child with ASC) looks after it and makes sure the symbols are taken off and posted away into a 'finished' pocket or box.

Symbols can read horizontally or vertically and their size can be adapted for individual childs' needs and abilities. Symbol-based timetables grow with the child, helping them to develop independence as they manage the information themselves. When the child can read more or cope with more information, then the timetable can be adjusted accordingly. Often this will be with more printed words and smaller symbols or pictures. It is good to continue the practice of managing their own timetable as they move into upper KS2 in order to increase their independence and prepare them for the transition to secondary school.

4 Written timetables

Some children with ASC may prefer a written list of the day's routine and schedule. This can be done on a whiteboard or in a notebook. Continue to mark which activities have finished by wiping them off the board, ticking them off or crossing them out.

Aim to have a Y5–6 children with ASC managing a whole week's timetable if they can, so that they are prepared for using a secondary school timetable, which will be their primary means of organisation when they move to KS3. As with all timetables, the rest of a primary class can benefit from learning these same organisation and self-checking skills.

There are many sources of free visual timetable symbols online (e.g. the TES and Do2Learn websites). Some sites such as Twinkl charge a small subscription. Purchased symbol software from Widgit™ and Boardmaker™ gives the buyer the flexibility to make their own bespoke timetables and schedules whenever needed. Choose simple symbols or pictures that the child with ASC can understand and relate to. Some children like to draw their own pictures and line drawings can be preferred by others.

Visual support for learning and other activities

Visual support can be used to structure and communicate in many areas. Usually, if a child isn't able to remember something or has difficulty understanding, a visual support can be a useful when used alongside other strategies.

Visual support can be used for:

- teaching self-help skills (e.g. for the morning routine, changing for PE, toileting, how to do something new).
- new experiences and change.
- making choices.
- expressing needs, wants, opinions, preferences and emotions.
- behaviour reminders and motivation.
- safety.

All the ideas in this chapter are suitable for children of any age and can easily be adapted for different abilities. See Chapter 5 for more about helping children with ASC to access the curriculum.

Visual support in the Early Years

In the Early Years, a child with ASC has a lot to learn about how to be at school. Routines and behaviours that children learn quickly from watching others can be difficult for children with ASC to grasp. They may not follow set routines (from hanging up their coat to sitting on the carpet for a story). They may not spend much time on one activity and flit from one area of the classroom to another. Conversely, they may spend all their time with one activity and find it difficult to share toys and attention with others. They may cry or have tantrums at lots of seemingly minor events, such as not being first, or when something unexpected happens.

In truth, the school world is likely to be a mass of confusing, overwhelming and terrifying demands for children with ASC. The only way they may be able to cope is to do their own thing and avoid difficult situations. Using visual supports like sequencing cards can help make sense of the world for these young children and teach them how to manage each situation so that it becomes familiar and predictable for them.

In order to develop their skills and abilities, it may be necessary to provide visual support for a range of school routines. These may include:

- using the toilet
- sitting on the carpet
- what to do in each activity
- lining up
- snack routines
- eating lunch
- getting changed for PE
- putting shoes on the right feet
- tidying up
- home time routine.

 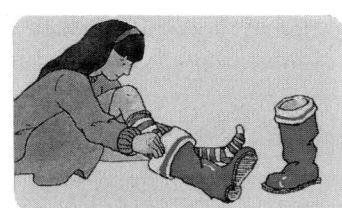 

Sequencing cards can help children learn routines.

Match these to the needs of individual children and their communication ability. It is important not to overwhelm the child by attempting to teach them too many things at once; it is always best to work through one skill at a time. Back-chaining can be a good way to teach a skill and ensure that the child has grasped each step. This involves doing each step with the child until they can do the last step on their own, then increasing that to them being able to do the last two steps on their own and so on, until the child feels confident with all the steps and can do them independently.

Case study

Mohammed (Reception pupil) was unable to feed himself when he came to school and his parents asked for help to teach him this skill. A visual schedule with the symbols for *hold spoon, pick up food, put in mouth, chew, well done,* and *do it again* was prepared and the teachers and parents back-chained the steps with him until he could do them all himself. In two weeks he was confidently feeding himself and trying new foods that he had previously avoided because he didn't know how to eat them without an adult feeding him.

Visual support in KS1

As children with ASC move into KS1, they may need continued support for early skills beyond that required for their peers. If they are able to access learning activities and classwork, they may also need visual supports to enable them to structure and organise their work.

There are many ways in which visual supports can be used to help a child learn new skills, access learning, develop independence and be able to deal with difficult situations. This can start with establishing attention. Use sensory objects, experiences or pictures to help the child focus on the topic you are teaching about. Let them hold things and match or sequence pictures to help them follow a story or topic. Story books lend themselves well to this and many have lots of great links to sensory experiences. Choose key parts of the story to introduce a new sensory experience and limit how many sensory experiences are given in one session. A great example is the story *We're going on a bear hunt*, which has clear sensory opportunities for the grass, water, mud and snow that the characters go through.

Visual supports can help children with ASC cope with the choices and demands they encounter each day. Think about using the following:

> A visual turn taking board. They may not understand sharing or like to do it but this resource can show them that they will soon have their go.

> A sand timer can show children how long the wait for their turn is, or how long is left of an activity before it will finish.

> First/Next schedule or a work time visual (if children are more able and beginning to sit at a table and do work activities) will help them know what the task is, and what is expected of them before they can do something else.

> A visual schedule can teach children to do jobs around the classroom such as giving things out, tidying up, or organising themselves at the end of the day.

> A visual review of the day can help parents know what the child has done at school each day.

> Visual reminders of the class rules and expected behaviours alongside personal behaviour charts can help and motivate a child with ASC, especially as it is clear, simple, visual and available.

> Traffic light cards and other communication cards can be used by a teaching assistant (TA) and child so they can communicate together without having to speak over the teacher during a class lesson.

Use a work time support so a child can see how the task is structured. See CD-ROM for printable work time visual support resource.

Work Time

First ➡ Count the beads

then ➡ write the number

finally ➡ do 5 more

I am working for _____
_____ playing bricks with a friend

Take care not to overload children with visuals, particularly about behaviour. Visual supports should allow the child with ASC to successfully negotiate the class routine, organise their things and do what they need to do to follow instructions and access learning. It is best to support one skill or task so that the child can do it well before introducing a new skill.

Case study

Darren (Y2 pupil) had a photograph of his neatest handwriting on his desk which helped him to keep his work neat and presentable each day. He felt very proud of his handwriting after that and understood how it helped his teacher read it more easily.

Visual support in KS2

In KS2, we should be mindful of building the organisation and independence skills of children with ASC so that they have the abilities and confidence they need to do things for themselves. It is good to work with parents at all stages throughout primary school, but especially in KS2 when children will be learning wider skills to help them in many different contexts. **See CD-ROM for a home–school communication template.**

- Visual sequences and lists can teach vital self-help skills (e.g. for dressing, personal hygiene, working with others on a shared task, doing jobs, and knowing how and when to ask for help).
- Children who find it difficult to remember things can write reminders on a mini-whiteboard or sticky notes.
- Mind maps can be used to help a child 'see' a whole situation or to understand how all the elements of a lesson topic fit together. They are very useful as reminders of new vocabulary and concepts related to a topic. Children can fill mind maps as a topic is studied, which will show the both the teacher and the child how much they are learning.
- Problem-solving can be supported visually. By mapping out what a problem is, a child can better understand what is going on and either offer or be offered some solutions. This can help the child see that they have choices and are able to contribute to the solution. **See CD-ROM for problem solving map.**
- Social stories™ (see Chapter 8) are a great way to visually represent a skill, experience or situation in order to help a child with ASC understand it.

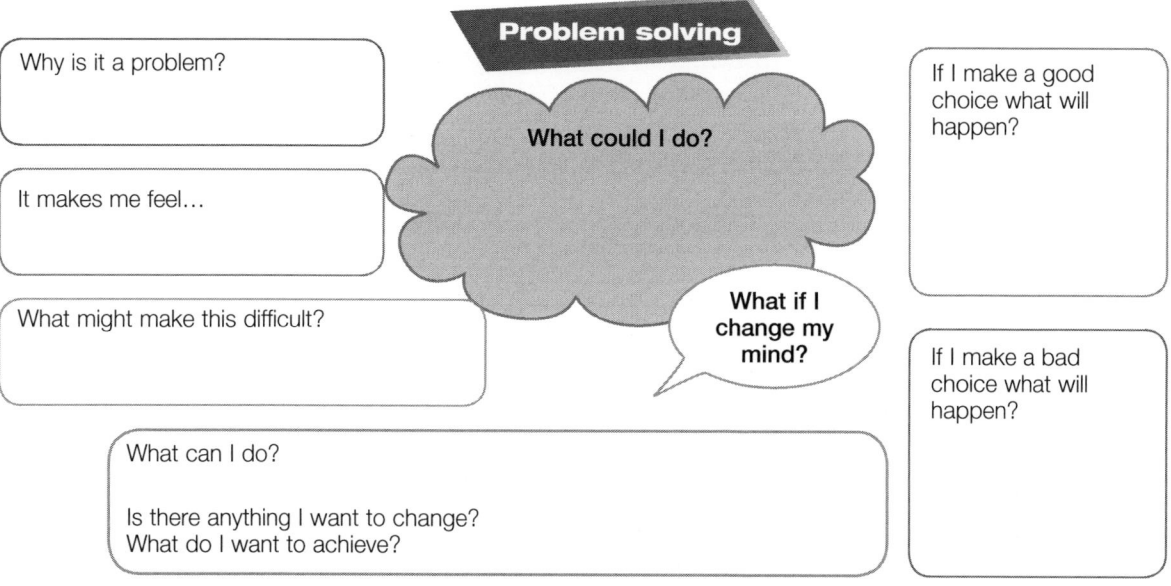

Problem solving map, See CD-ROM for printable resource.

Visual behaviour support

Behaviour that is of concern (such as fiddling, being distracted and/or distracting others, refusal, running away, confrontation, self-harming) or any behaviour that restricts a child with ASC from learning means that they are communicating that something is not working for them. They may be confused, frustrated, overwhelmed or need help.

Children with ASC can also miss many of the cues about expected behaviour that their peers will naturally pick up. A *Golden Rules* poster on the wall, non-verbal communication from the teacher and following what everyone else is doing may work for some children, but might not for children with ASC.

Children with ASC may have a slower processing ability, resulting in them missing all or parts of verbal instructions and behaviour directions. They will often not respond when everyone else does because they are still trying to process the language long after.

A child with ASC who finds school confusing and overwhelming may also seem to want to 'do their own thing' or control what others are doing. They may be trying to avoid or seek out sensory experiences to enable them to regulate their own systems, resulting in unexpected and/or unwanted behaviour.

Behaviour expectations and reward charts can be helpful, particularly when they are linked to a child's particular interests. To make rewards achievable, ensure that the child with ASC knows what the expectations are clearly and logically. All rules should be telling children what we *do* want them to do, rather than what we *don't* want them to do. This can prevent much of our communication with them from becoming too negative.

Case study

Ayesha (Y5 pupil) had a visual reminder that she could talk about her favourite subject, which was dinosaurs, only after she had finished her work.

I can talk about dinosaurs

Time: _____

Until: _____

Remember to try to think and talk about the lesson topic when you are in class.

A tangible reward or a points system where a child earns rewards over a period of time can work for some children. Any sanctions should be made explicitly clear, preferably visually, and the child should be able to understand what they are and why they are getting the sanction.

CHAPTER 5
Accessing the curriculum

From Early Years to the end of KS2, the school day is planned, directed and assessed in terms of childrens' learning, and how they explain, show and record what they are learning. All children must follow the National Curriculum and be assessed against demanding targets. The Education Act (2011) gave all children the right to a broad and balanced curriculum, and the data collection that each school is bound to report includes all children.

The Children and Families Act (2014) and the subsequent SEND Code of Practice (2014) stipulate that class teachers are responsible for the progress of all the children in their class, including those with SEND. Teachers spend hours planning lessons for different subjects that engage children and differentiate for all the abilities and needs within one class. The difficulty for a mainstream teacher is that there is often a lack of training about SEND in general, and Autism Spectrum Condition (ASC) in particular. Despite this, they are still expected to be responsible for meeting all childrens' needs.

Some teachers have teaching assistants (TAs) and some do not. Some children have one-to-one support allocated to them, but many do not. This chapter will look at how teachers can approach teaching and support the learning of children with ASC and will give some tips on how best to use TAs if they are available.

Teaching and learning in the Early Years

You may have a child starting in the Early Years who already has a diagnosis of ASC. More commonly, the difficulties associated with ASC may be picked up by staff in the Early Years classroom. They may have noticed differences in a child's behaviour and responses, communication, social interaction, flexible thinking and sensory processing.

The way to engage a child with ASC in the Early Years curriculum is through play. However, because of their condition, a child with ASC may have very different play patterns and purposes to other children. Observe and get to know the child, speak to parents and gather information about which areas of the classroom the child goes to, what they do when they are there, what interests them (in the environment, as well as the classroom activities) and what kind of play or exploration they engage in.

Supporting play in the Early Years

Once you have identified the characteristics of a child's interactions and play, you should know what motivates and interests them. Begin with what the child is doing and engage them in shared experiences through imitation and enticement. Supported play sessions are most useful with children who have delayed development, poor play and language skills and need a lot of support to access the early years activities and environment. Recommendations for supporting play sessions:

1 **Set the scene**
   Use a defined area for the play activity such as a mat, play tray, or table. Remove all objects not associated with the play from the play area if possible to help focus attention.

2 **Play partners**
   When a child with ASC seems not to engage with others you may need to engage with them first. Plan to use what interests and motivates the child to establish the play relationship and shared attention with the play partner (teaching staff). Put the play items in the defined area and where possible have two of each so the play partner can imitate the child's play and model to the child different ways of playing, rather than take an object off them to show them something new.

3 **Keep it short**
   It is better to have a short, pleasurable, interactive session and let the child indicate when they have had enough, than to force the child to continue under duress. If short and positive experiences happen throughout the day, children with ASC will be motivated to seek out adults to play with and will understand that interacting can be shared and fun. The duration of the activities will then begin to extend.

Staff training

Train all adults in the setting in autism awareness for Early Years, and train them to follow the play sessions approaches above, allowing each adult to do a short play session with the child each day. This will enable the child with ASC to learn how to interact with different people who are consistent in approach.

Introducing peer play

Once the child is engaging in regular and positive play sessions with adults, then you can bring another child alongside them and show them how to play with the child with ASC in a similar manner. This works best when only one other child at a time is involved. Teaching other children to engage with the child with ASC (particularly if they are non-verbal) in this way can lead to good mutual relationships and friendships as the children grow up together. Choose children who have similar interests, and those with an interest in the child with ASC to begin with. Always let the child with ASC be involved in their choice of play partner.

Watch and praise

Observe and encourage any positive interactions between the child with ASC and other children. Praise both parties and tell them specifically what they were doing well (e.g. *'That was good turn-taking.'*).

Play for play's sake

When setting up play activities, don't strive for a particular learning outcome. Of course, you will be looking for evidence of learning and development, but if you are flexible you will be able to find this when you think about the wider picture. It may be that children are learning something completely different than what you intended, but that is still valuable to the child and can be recorded in a different area of the Early Years Foundation Stage (EYFS) curriculum.

It can be difficult to organise structured play sessions in an Early Years classroom when everything is always out and available. There are examples of excellent practice where Early Years classrooms have been rearranged and organised around the needs of children with ASC. By having less toys out at once and rotating the activities and toys that are available, children can spend longer in constructive play and learning. Less choice can be very beneficial for children with ASC. This can benefit all children in providing a calm and structured classroom.

When children with ASC have a peer play partner, include activities like action songs, rhymes, games, cause and effect toys, turn-taking games, sensory toys, tickle games and passing activities to encourage communication and social interaction. If a child with ASC is relatively confident and tolerant of others, do these activities in a small group of about four children. Structure the session by putting it onto a visual timetable with symbols or photos for the breakdown of the session.

Structured activities for learning in the Early Years

A child with ASC may not be interested in new activities that require them to practise a skill they have not yet mastered. They could communicate this through their behaviour (e.g. they may seem disinterested or distressed, or refuse to do the activity). Teaching a child with ASC how to approach a new learning activity may therefore need to be planned and structured carefully. If the child has difficulty imagining the outcome of the activity, how long it will last and/or what it is you want them to do, then they will resist what might be a simple and engaging activity for many children.

Children with ASC must be given a clear structure and guidelines for doing expected activities so that they know:

- **what** they have to do
- **why** they are doing it
- **how** much they have to do
- **when** it will be finished
- **what** will happen next

The best activities are structured so well that the child has all the above questions answered.

Recommendations

- Give the child everything they need for a task in a plastic folder or tray, box or basket (e.g. for a cutting and sticking activity add scissors and glue; for a jigsaw, put all the pieces in a tray or clear bag).
- Have a clear place to put the task when it is finished (e.g. a 'finished' tray on the table). This can be a good strategy for tidying up too.
- Use the child's interests where possible. For example, if it is dinosaurs, count dinosaurs, have dinosaur-themed alphabets, dinosaur colours, dinosaur books to look at, or dinosaur outlines on worksheets.
- Make the work achievable. The first time you do an activity, it might be a good idea to give the child nearly completed work so that they can easily be successful. Increase the amount to complete next time (another example of back-chaining).
- Vary the type of activities to cover the full range of early learning skills. But remember, small but regular successes are better than forcing longer engagement.
- These strategies all have the advantage of helping a child with ASC learn to do activities independently. An adult can introduce the activity but the child should be able to 'see' what they have to do and be successful in doing the activity independently.

➤ For ideas for visual and structured tasks, search online for *TEACCH tasks* or *visual work tasks*.

Teaching and learning in KS1

As children with ASC move into Y1 and Y2, it is essential to have a joined-up and long-term plan for developing their learning and skills. Children with ASC may be working at a level below the National Curriculum and so may need to be assessed according to the P scales or the pre-national curriculum assessment that will replace these in the near future. If a child is at this level, it is important that the class teacher familiarises themselves with these so that the child's learning needs can be planned for.

Children with ASC may have age-appropriate academic ability or have co-morbid learning disabilities. If they are working significantly below the expected levels for their age, then it is important to check that they are being given academic work to do, that teaches them the skills and concepts that they need. A watered-down version of what the rest of the class is doing is not appropriate if the child needs more work on the key learning that the majority of the class has already attained. These key areas of learning may need to form the child's Individual Education Plan (IEP) and may become part of their Education, Health and Care (EHC) Plan, if applied for. The class teacher will need to reflect this in their planning and communication to the support staff, the child's individual objectives for each lesson, or how the class objective is going to be differentiated.

Case study

Ali (Y2 pupil) was working below the National Curriculum expected level for Y1 maths. He was stronger in numbers and functions but was being held back by his difficulty in using and applying number concepts, and his inability to solve even the simplest word problems.

Using the P scale descriptors, his teacher assessed the gaps in his learning and identified that he had not understood the basic maths concept words, and that this had not been revisited. Using visual supports, he was taught these concept words and helped to apply them to his maths work. Ali learned the vocabulary and was able to make good progress, catching up with his peers.

Workstations in KS1

A structured, step-by-step work system with a screen, often on a separate table, is frequently recommended for a child with ASC, but it is important to be clear about why you are going to use one and how it will benefit the child.

Spending the school day working on a table in a corridor is not good practice and does not include the child in mainstream schooling. A workstation is usually at a desk in the classroom and is intended to help the child learn how to work, how to organise that work and what to do when it is finished. The work system can be on a separate table, often with a three-sided privacy screen or by a plain wall, minimising distractions and visually indicating to the child that it is 'work time'. This can improve a child's concentration and motivation and reduce any anxiety they have about doing schoolwork. Subsequently, behaviours they may engage in to avoid doing 'work' can be avoided.

A work system teaches a left-to-right structure with a clear starting and finishing place. There can be more than one numbered activity to be 'collected' from the left (magazine boxes, baskets, trays can all be used) and plastic pockets can be used to put all the equipment needed for the activity in. For example, for a system showing three tasks to complete: each task should be placed in a folder in the box to the left of the child. The child can collect the first task, complete it, and put it into the 'finished' place, which is the box to the right. It is important to teach the child the concept of 'finished', and this will give them a sense of achievement.

Using this system, children know exactly how much work there is to do. They would usually have a reward activity to do once all work is completed. This can build their motivation to engage in learning activities and help the child develop a sense of purpose, develop their organisation skills and develop the ability to work independently. If a child learns success through using a workstation they will be more ready to use those skills when working on a group table alongside other children.

The next step is to transfer the work system onto a regular class table and slowly take away the boxes or baskets at either side. It is important to still have a clear 'start' and 'finish' to every task and it can be beneficial for all children to have a 'finished' box in the middle of their table. This can help children who are academically able but unable to complete a task independently without a lot of adult help and prompting. A work system replaces the adult prompting and provides a clear visual structure that children with ASC can follow much more easily.

A good way to develop this idea when moving on is to use a **work time visual support on the CD-ROM**. This uses the same principle of starting, organising and finishing a piece of work.

Teaching and learning in KS2

Children with ASC can be very able academically but still have many challenges to overcome in accessing the curriculum and completing classwork to the expected standard. Difficulties with understanding verbal communication, executive functioning (i.e. planning, organising, monitoring and focusing), sensory distortion and overload, rigid thinking and obsessive interests can impact on their ability to engage with classwork.

Some children with ASC excel at certain subjects, but there are likely to be other subjects that they do not enjoy and find very difficult to engage with. Other children with ASC will still be struggling to manage the increased sensory input in the school environment. Many have difficulty making links and generalising what they have learned, which greatly impacts on their attainment. Some children with ASC will be working at a much lower level than the rest of their peers right through KS2 and may still be working within the P scales or the pre-national curriculum assessment that will replace these in the near future. However, if children with ASC are given the support they need, they can be more successful in their academic achievements. The end goal is to develop more independent working for these children, but this may take some time and consistency to achieve.

Case study

Kiera (Y3 pupil) had a full time TA as she was unable to access much of the work that the class were doing. The teacher was struggling to differentiate the work she had planned, which was based on the Y3 curriculum. She realised that Kiera needed a personalised curriculum based on the Y1 learning objectives as she needed to learn earlier skills and concepts. Using the National Curriculum for Y1, the teacher and TA were able to engage Kiera in the topic that the class were learning but provide differentiated work at the right level for her.

Accessing learning in KS2

Much of the teaching done in KS2 is verbal. Teachers talk, explain, instruct, ask questions and encourage whole class discussions. This is done with the assumption that children have reached a certain level of development in their understanding and ability to communicate. The teacher expects children to understand basic concepts, be able to think about abstract ideas and take on board a variety of perspectives. They will expect that most children can compose different pieces of writing such as a report, story, account or instructions. They will expect children to be able to ask and answer questions, draw conclusions, and understand sarcasm and jokes and where to 'draw the line'.

Of course, teachers understand that in every class there will be children who struggle with some of these abilities. For children with ASC, verbal communication can be difficult to understand, keep up with and contribute to. Children with ASC may speak fluently and use long words, but their speech may be rambling, lacking in clarity of purpose and direction. They may want to speak only about things important to themselves and need help to learn about appropriate speech, tone and volume. They may interrupt, call out or argue that others are saying the wrong things, or they may be too quiet and reluctant to speak in class at all. There are many issues that can affect a child with ASC. These include:

- Difficulties 'tuning in' to the teacher when there is background noise, flickering lights, or others moving about the room. For children who experience sensory processing difficulties, these distractions can make them feel stressed and unable to concentrate. Try to sit them where distractions are minimal and teach all the class to be calm and quiet when you are speaking to them.

- Difficulties keeping up with the pace of spoken communication, such as the number of instructions given out before starting a piece of work. Children with ASC will have a slower processing time, meaning that they can be still trying to understand the first thing you said, when you have moved on to the next instruction or further examples.

- Difficulty understanding the inferred and assumed meaning of what has been said, especially if using sarcasm or jokes. Explain to children what sarcasm and jokes are and don't use sarcasm when speaking directly to a child with ASC – you may be taken literally.

- Difficulty looking at the teacher at the same time as listening. Teachers will usually expect children to show that they are listening by looking at them. Some children with ASC cannot do both and so if you insist on them looking at you, this takes so much concentration that they are unable to process what they are listening to. Allow the child to look elsewhere but check that they are listening through questioning and bringing them into the discussion through practical activities.

- Difficulty understanding what the important part of the information they are being told is. They may not be able to see the 'big picture', instead becoming overwhelmed with irrelevant details. A TA writing key words on a whiteboard or having visual pictures of the topic can bring them in to the discussion, and these can be taken back to the child's table to support their work.

- Difficulty in being verbally able to ask for help. This often causes children with ASC to sit not doing anything for long periods of time. It might help to invent a secret sign for children to make so that no-one but the teacher knows they need help (e.g. putting a pencil on the end of their table). A traffic light code can be used to indicate what stage they are at (green = *'I'm okay.'*, amber = *'I'm trying it myself.'*, red = *'I need help.'*).

Many of the strategies used for supporting KS1 children with ASC to access the curriculum and learn to do things for themselves are still applicable at KS2. Teachers should aim to develop a child's independence so that some support can be withdrawn but be wary of stopping strategies that have worked, especially when the child is moving from one class to another at the end of the year. It can be that children who don't seem to rely on a particular support (e.g. a visual timetable) begin to display behaviour difficulties when it is taken away, often showing us that the presence of the support was more important to the child than was realised.

Support in curriculum subjects

English

Reading

Every child with ASC will be different in their ability to learn to read through phonics or other methods. Some may be able to read before they start school; others will be unable to articulate letter sounds because of their speech and communication difficulties. However, do not assume that a non-verbal child cannot understand written words. Some children with ASC can read but not speak.

Some children with ASC will struggle with phonics, being able to learn letter names and sounds but struggling to blend them and move on from Stage 2 of phonics. This can greatly impair their reading development. Despite the need to test and report on phonics, children with ASC may need more time learning sight words and support to understand what they are reading. If learning phonics does not work for the child, look at supporting them by developing their reading skills using other methods. Some approaches recommended for children with ASC include:

- ► A multi-sensory approach including auditory, visual and tactile experiences. Some children love learning phonics through ICT, apps and songs.
- ► Be flexible and try different methods such as whole-word recognition. This works well with symbols, which help a child understand the word they are reading.

Teachers need to check reading comprehension skills in children with ASC. These children can easily misunderstand a text, take what they read literally, or read fluently without understanding the text or being able to recall what they read at all. Reading comprehension skills will need supporting with inference and narrative skills (being able to tell a story or account of an event in a structured way), as well as help with social understanding.

A child with ASC may find fiction does not make sense to them because they do not understand the social implications in the story. They may need targeted support to help them learn about inference and 'making guesses' based on the clues in the text. Regular comprehension exercises on short pieces of text can help improve their understanding.

Even choosing a book from the school library can be overwhelming for a child with ASC because there is too much choice. If a child refuses to read, it is a good idea to give them a box of books to choose from which includes books they have read before, factual books on their particular interests, comics and graphic books, and a few new books that may have a connection to something they are interested in.

Writing

Some children with ASC can write well and compose imaginative stories, full of great ideas. However, these children often share common difficulties when it comes to mark-making and writing. They often have difficulties with executive functioning skills (i.e. the thinking skills that help the brain organise and act on information). These enable children to plan, organise, remember things, prioritise, self-monitor, pay attention, use information and experiences from the past to solve current problems, and know how to start activities. These are important skills in composing a piece of writing.

Children with ASC can be affected by four major difficulties when it comes to writing:

1 Motor skills

Children with ASC may have difficulty with fine motor skills and handwriting, sometimes being unable to hold and manipulate a pencil. Poor handwriting can be linked to differences in sensory sensitivity (such as how much pressure to put on the pencil) and the brain having difficulty with motor planning (Fuentes, Mostofsky & Bastian, 2009).

The best support for children with ASC is to provide structured handwriting practice in short, daily sessions. Set out clearly what and how much the child has to do and make the content interesting to them (e.g. words or sentences based on their interests). They can also be taught to use technology alongside handwriting, and be allowed the use of typing for longer pieces. They may need to practise exercises and sensory activities to improve their grasp and motor processing.

2 Composition

A child's ability to compose a story or piece of writing depends on their ability to imagine things that don't happen in reality or what something will be like and use words and phrases to bring those ideas to an audience. As common features of ASC are language impairment and difficulty in understanding other people's ideas, motivations and thoughts, composing a piece of writing, especially creative writing, often seems an impossible task for a child with the condition. Their writing may look very similar to a story they already know, such as a film script. Support children by making the task about the composition rather than the handwriting. If needed, let an adult scribe or the child use a computer or dictation app to record the story or account.

3 Organisation

Using visual cues to help the child organise their writing can be very helpful. Writing frames, chunking work so that children only see one section at a time and clear worksheets (with all non-essential pictures or information taken off) work well, as do the other supports for organisation and independence outlined in this book.

4 Anxiety

A child with ASC can have great fear and anxiety about writing. They can be afraid of making mistakes, not understanding how to check and correct them, and not wanting to have to go over a task they consider finished again. Having to think about organisation, composition and motor skills involved can be too much for them to cope with and lead to a refusal to do the writing task at all. Their anxiety can lead to challenging avoidance behaviour. Support children with ASC by focusing on their successes, and explain that making and correcting mistakes is part of learning.

Anxiety can be reduced through achievable tasks that are well structured and linked to a child's interests. Try focusing on just one of the four writing skills at a time so that the child can develop each one individually and then bring them together. This works best when it is planned and monitored in an IEP or similar document.

Case study

Michael (Y4 pupil) was refusing to write anything at all. He would tear up his paper, run out of class or throw objects whenever he was asked to write. He was rarely in the classroom and his peer relationships were breaking down at break times because he was finding everything about school stressful and overwhelming, due to not wanting to write. Michael was assessed for handwriting and motor skills, and was asked about his anxiety levels and thoughts about writing, and what he was interested in. His teacher put a structured programme together in very small, achievable steps (see below). Michael needed support for his anxiety and so motivations such as stickers and praise were important for his success. This programme took two terms to achieve. By the end of it, Michael also achieved being in class working with his peers full time.

My writing plan		
	Step	**Support**
1	I will try to write two sentences about my favourite subject every day.	My teaching assistant will use pictures and help me think of sentences to write. I will choose a sticker to put on my achievement chart.
2	I will try to write between three and five sentences about my favourite subject every day. This will make a paragraph.	My teaching assistant will use pictures to help me sequence my sentences and I will choose a sticker to put on my achievement chart.
3	I will try to write between one and two paragraphs about my favourite subject every day.	My teaching assistant will use pictures to help me sequence my sentences and I will try to write independently. I will choose a sticker to put on my achievement chart.
4	I will try to write between one and two paragraphs about a different subject of my choice every day.	Pictures will be available about different things I can write about and I will try to start my writing independently. I can ask if I need help. I will choose a sticker to put on my achievement chart.
5	I will try to write between one and two paragraphs on my teacher's choice of subject on two days, and my subject of choice the other days.	Pictures will be available about things I can write about. My teaching assistant will talk through what I have learned about the subject and help me make notes. I will try to start my writing independently and ask if I need help. I will choose a sticker to put on my achievement chart.

Maths

Some children with ASC are very good at maths. Often, they like the structured and logical nature of the subject and quickly see patterns and connections in numbers, shapes and measures. Others struggle to grasp maths concepts or apply their numerical knowledge to number word problems. Their communication difficulties may impair their ability to follow instructions and understand complex explanations.

Number

Numbers and the number operations may be far easier to learn for children with ASC than other children because they are logical, structured and systematic. Indeed, some children with ASC are so good at number operations that they can be way ahead of their peers, and some are even so good that difficulties arise when they are asked to show their working out. For a child who just 'knows' the answer, this seems unnecessary and they may struggle to backtrack the thinking process to be able to explain it to someone else. Other children with ASC find maths difficult from the start and may need support to learn the basics. As with many children, failure to grasp the early concepts can lead to a child's refusal to believe that maths is a subject they are good at or able to achieve in.

Recommendations:

➤ Where possible, give one instruction at a time and make sure that explanations are supported visually or practically.

➤ Help children to become familiar with number. For example, use numerals on visual schedules and make lists of tasks using numbers. Parents can support this through counting and pointing out numbers at home.

➤ With younger children, look at TEACCH maths ideas for ideas on how to present maths activities in structured and visual formats which encourage independent learning.

➤ Support maths through visual and multi-sensory activities. Help children develop early maths concepts by explaining what the concepts are and, using this vocabulary, give them opportunities for 'real-life' maths practice (e.g. shopping, building, giving things out in class, finding things). As with all activities, use a child's special interests where possible.

➤ Use ICT and apps to support maths learning. These can be very motivating for children with ASC.

➤ Children with ASC may have visual perception difficulties which can cause them to find shapes and space difficult to recognise and work with. Others may have a real strength in understanding the features, properties and concepts of shape and space. For those who have difficulty, the key is to break down and structure activities, check understanding and support children with practical and visual activities.

➤ Recognising shapes in the environment may be a strength in some children with ASC who notice detail, but others may not be able to generalise so easily. Some children with ASC will not have the flexibility of thought to do this and so it will take more structured and repetitive teaching to embed the concepts of shape, space and measure that they need to learn.

Using and applying maths

This is about using maths to solve everyday problems. Often, children with ASC may find this difficult because they are presented with a word problem on a worksheet, and may not make the connection between the word problem and the real-life situations that require maths knowledge or skills. Basically, children with ASC need to see the point of what you are asking them to do.

Recommendations:

➤ When introducing maths word problems, begin with ones that are simple and logical and do not have lots of unrelated information in them. If it helps, make them about the child's special interests to motivate them.

➤ You can support children with ASC with practical problems by using a maths vocabulary keyring, or having the visual vocabulary on a prompt sheet beside them. Get in the habit of asking the child to find the maths function the problem is asking them to do. As they get older and begin to attempt word problems, they can use a highlighter to identify key words.

➤ Explain and describe how you are using maths in all activities. Use a social story to teach children why working out needs to be shown and teach them how to do this. Some children with ASC who are very able at maths will find this a difficult issue to overcome.

➤ Homework activities can focus on the practical use of maths. Older children can do practical tasks that involve numbers such as shopping, counting pocket money, telling the time and baking with their parents.

PE

Some children with ASC enjoy the physical nature of PE and seek to run off their pent-up energy with glee. For those with good physical skills, this can be a relief from the stresses and demands of the classroom, particularly written work.

However, many children with ASC struggle greatly with PE. There are sensory challenges (e.g. getting changed into their PE kit, a large echoing hall, different textures and temperatures), lots of movement demands and instructions, activities needing co-operation and co-ordination, team games, turn-taking and winning and losing. These can all be very stressful for children with ASC. Other challenges for these children can also include:

➤ Communication difficulties. Understanding, remembering and processing instructions can be difficult and time-consuming for children with ASC. The other children may already have started an activity while a child with ASC is still processing the instruction. Use visuals and give instructions one at a time.

➤ Working as part of a team. It is better to allow children with ASC to work alone or with a sympathetic partner than in a group. Teach turn-taking and waiting, and praise them specifically when they do this well. Work out who will be a child's partner in advance rather than giving a free choice during the session.

➤ Activities such as passing a ball may be difficult for children with poor eye contact skills. Support children before this kind of activity with following/tracking activities (e.g. to see where a rolled ball goes). For team games, explain the point of the game carefully and look at video clips to support this.

➤ The lack of physical boundaries in large spaces such as playing fields can cause great anxiety, or be seen as licence to run free! Children with ASC can also find it hard to find a space to sit in. Use cones, spot markers and other visual clues to help them understand boundaries, routes and directions.

➤ Poor awareness of personal space and appropriate touch may need specific teaching, visual support and social stories to explain. Games such as *Traffic Lights* (where children run around and respond to simple instructions such as *stop, go, skip,* and *hop*) can help children with ASC learn about when to stop, when to go and how to avoid others when running around.

➤ Sensitivity to noise in an echoing sports hall or the smell of sweaty bodies or food smells immediately after lunch can be overwhelming. Children with ASC may need to wear ear defenders, and you may need to seek to change your PE session to the morning or later in the afternoon.

➤ Difficulty in using their imagination may affect a child's creativity in dance or gymnastics. Give children with ASC pictures of moves to copy. These can be found from a variety of sources, including some free online (such as on the Sparklebox website).

➤ A new routine or activity can be stressful for children with ASC as they may not know what the point of the activity is. Prepare the child by showing them what you will be doing first, or by using a social story (see Chapter 8).

➤ Poor body awareness can prevent a child with ASC understanding and communicating how their body feels during different activities. They can be prone to over-heating or being cold without being aware of it.

PSHE

This area of the curriculum is non-statutory but represents all the core areas of weakness for children with ASC. Schools should make provision for PSHE, which includes sex and relationships education, and will need to take into account the needs of children with ASC when doing so. Social communication, awareness of others, awareness of their community, personal development, belonging and friendships will be important topics for children with ASC, and PSHE targets should be part of their Individual Education Plan (IEP). See Chapter 10 for ideas to support children in PSHE, and with social interaction and skills.

Other areas of the curriculum

Every child with ASC will enjoy some subject areas and dislike others. They may have an uneven academic profile and be more inspired by subjects that are practical, artistic, scientific or related to their special interests. The changes to the National Curriculum in 2015 mean children are required to learn a demanding amount in all subjects at a faster pace than ever. Pressure to have evidence and to be able to record their knowledge is enormous, and any difficulty with communication, social interaction, flexible thinking and sensory processing is going to have an impact on a child with ASC's ability to access the curriculum. The testing and assessment regime will be another challenge that may cause anxiety, distress and difficulties for children with ASC.

There are often far more barriers to learning for a child with ASC than a neurotypical child. Overcoming the difficulties they may have in English and maths will underpin their success in many other subjects. Indeed, they may excel in subjects that they understand, like and feel successful in. Imaginative teachers can often find a 'way in' for even their most reluctant children once they understand their needs. Outdoor learning, ICT and practical activities can be used in many imaginative ways to support the curriculum.

Strengths and difficulties children with ASC commonly have in their school subjects

Science

Strengths	Difficulties
Children with ASC often have a strong interest in and aptitude for science. Science is about logical and systematic processes, practical experiments and factual knowledge. Children who love science can be supported to look at other subjects in a scientific way. You may have a child who has superior scientific knowledge (more than the curriculum demands). Some children with ASC may be extremely gifted and talented in science and should be supported to extend and widen their knowledge, skills and understanding of the subject.	Children with poor executive functioning can struggle to follow instructions and carry out an experiment that requires them to draw conclusions from their investigations. They can easily lose where they are up to and will need visual and structured support to be able to carry out an activity. If they are very poor at drawing conclusions, they may need to choose from two or three alternatives where only one is likely. Teaching the concepts of *likely* and *unlikely* can also be useful. There may also be some issues with sensory processing in science, so do be aware of issues regarding food, smells, texture, touch, movement and visual focus. If a child is refusing to take part, check that you have prepared them for what is happening, communicated this appropriately to them and considered their sensory profile when planning practical science activities.

History and Geography

Strengths	Difficulties
These may be subjects that are closely related to a child with ASC's special interests. The factual aspect of these subjects may also appeal to them; some children with ASC can memorise huge amounts of factual, historical or geographical data (such as a list of all the British Prime Ministers, or types of rocks and gems). However, in history and geography children with ASC may need many opportunities to put the factual information they know into meaningful context and be able to 'see' how particular events, people or systems fit together. This can be done through timelines, mind maps, video clips, pictures and diagrams.	Some children with ASC may find the concept of time very difficult to grasp, both in terms of ordering events in the past, and in imagining what an unfamiliar place or environment might be like. They may also need support in the organisation and imagination required to write about unfamiliar concepts and events. Children who find English tasks difficult may resist more writing during topic time. Help children with ASC to engage with these subjects through visuals, practical experiences, roleplay, school visits, pictures and ICT. It may help to structure a lesson using a visual timetable, and make timelines and diagrams in a way that the child contributes to and understands. These should have reference points and start with things that are familiar to them. Children can then add the new information in in relation to that. Children with ASC may need support to reflect on the meaning of events and consider their impact and different points of view surrounding them.

Design Technology (DT) and ICT

Strengths	Difficulties
Children with ASC are often extremely proficient at using technology and can become very competent with computers, tablets or laptops. They may also have practical skills in construction and design ideas and be artistic which can mean that DT and ICT are successful areas of the curriculum for them.	Children with ASC may need support to follow stepped instructions and can easily rush ahead as they get involved in practical or computer-based tasks or activities without reflecting on what they are being asked to do. Use a 'Work Time' visual support (see photocopiable resource on accompanying CD-ROM) to explain the steps of the task before you begin and identify specific points during the task for the child to stop, report, reflect, record or wait for teacher input. Sensory or motor difficulties can be a barrier to doing practical DT tasks and teachers should be aware of children with ASC's needs and abilities. Some children find the design process too hard and will therefore refuse to begin. It can be useful to support them with a choice of pictures and visual ideas to begin with, rather than asking them to create something from scratch. When using computers, children with ASC can easily become fixated on what they want to do or a game they want to play and ignore what they have been asked to do. They can also find it difficult to share a computer or work on a joint task with another child as the social communication demands, paired with the task demands, may be overwhelming. Support children with structure, small steps, good communication and tangible rewards. It is a good idea to teach 'work time' and 'game time' on the computer as separate activities from the early years.

Music

Strengths	Difficulties
Children with ASC can respond positively to music and some have good rhythm, fluency and aptitude in the subject. They can follow the structured elements of musical patterns and can have good musicality. They may have a good singing voice and a memory for lyrics and notation. Some will have an 'ear' for playing musical instruments and follow musical notation well. Practising and performing music along with their peers can develop social confidence, and learning an instrument can develop skills outside having to write and remember facts and concepts. Joining a school choir or band can help with a child's social inclusion and build their confidence too.	Sound sensitivity will affect some children with ASC, especially when the class is composing their own music with a variety of instruments. (This can seem overwhelmingly noisy and chaotic.) They may be able to wear noise-reducing headphones, or you may need to make sure that you spread children out to different areas so that each group can hear themselves more clearly. Interpreting music may be difficult for children with ASC as they often have difficulty imagining what something will be like which may affect composition, communicating their ideas and guessing the meaning of a piece of music. If a child with ASC is struggling with these aspects of music, they can be given picture choices and listen to ideas from others before making their own choices.

Art & Design

Strengths	Difficulties
Some children with ASC can be brilliant artists and welcome the break from writing in other subjects. Art, and drawing in particular, can be a favourite activity of some children. Some have a strong (even photographic) visual memory, which can translate into detailed and accurate artistic representations. Children who cannot speak very well can immerse themselves in an artistic activity and produce work that does not have rigid outcomes and expectations. For some children with ASC, drawing can be a means of communication, taking the pressure off them to verbally articulate what they want to say.	When a child with ASC finds unstructured and open-ended activities overwhelming, art can be a subject with too little direction and children can be afraid of 'getting it wrong'. Being unable to generate ideas can prevent them from engaging in the activity. Other issues are sensory; texture and messiness can be too much for children to cope with and they can become very distressed. If a child with ASC is not engaging with art activities, begin with something they can do and will be successful at. Structure the steps of the activity and introduce sensory textures and activities slowly. Children may accept new experiences over time or flatly refuse because they cannot cope with the sensory experience. In this case, the activity should be adapted so that they can do something more tolerable for them. Watching someone else do the activity (via video clip or in person) so that they can replicate the activity can also help. Children with ASC may prefer to work alone rather than in a group and so paired or group working should be introduced with a lot of support, or it may be necessary that children with ASC are allowed to do their own piece of work.

Religious Education (RE)

Strengths	Difficulties
Children with ASC can be very attuned to aspects of faith and religion and find interest and comfort in the structure and routine of religious practices. If they are from a faith-practising family, they may be very familiar with some aspects that they are learning about and be able to speak about their own experiences.	Understanding abstract concepts may be difficult for children with ASC, and understanding other people's views and opinions when there is no right or wrong answer can cause confusion. Some children with ASC are literal and rigid in their opinions and find it difficult to accept the opinions of others. In subjects like RE, this can cause arguments and a refusal to engage with the work. Seeing the point of what they are doing is important to children with ASC, and RE can be difficult to explain at times. If a child does not have a personal belief, they may refuse to engage with the subject. Social stories can help children with ASC understand why people follow a religion and have faith.

Modern foreign language

Strengths	Difficulties
Many children with ASC can find the practical learning of a modern foreign language relatively easy. If they are good at rote learning, then the vocabulary and phrasing that they learn at primary level is practical and functional, and therefore makes sense to a logical ASC mind. Often teachers will use ICT or pictures to teach MFL, which plays to the learning strengths of children with ASC.	Children who have difficulty with their first language (with receptive and expressive communication) will find using language in social situations and knowing what to say and how to talk to others difficult in a second language. It may be that children with ASC need visuals or scripts to read to help them practise their MFL vocabulary. Putting language in a roleplay context (e.g. a French café) might help them see the purpose of the language.

Tests

Children in Reception, Y2 and Y6 will be preparing for national phonics screening and SATs, and children in other years may be assessed through optional SATs. If a child is considered unable to access a test (particularly if it is statutory), information about making the decision and applying for dispensations can be found on the UK Government website.

Many children with ASC have difficulties with attempting to do a test, including timing, the ability to concentrate, anxiety about getting it wrong, not understanding the language, a longer processing time and being literal in their understanding. For example:

> Q: *Can you tell me how the children got to the seaside?*
>
> A: *Yes.*

Therefore, if a child is at a level at which testing can be taught, they can be introduced to it by using a social story which should include what tests are for and how to go about doing them. However, tests (with their associated time constraints and pressure) may be overwhelming for a child with ASC and schools should take steps as early as possible to either prepare the child for them or make alternative arrangements.

You can teach test skills like any other skills, by breaking them into manageable chunks, starting with one section and adding another one as children develop confidence. With regular practice and support, children with ASC may be able to sit a whole test. Always monitor a child's ability to process the questions, ensuring that they understand correctly and not just literally what they are being asked. You may need to teach them how to interpret questions and what key phrases mean so that they do not always answer literally. Try to build upon their successes slowly, such as by reducing the amount of questions or doing half of the test one day and the other half the next. Failing to achieve or complete a test is likely to cause the child to not want to do them at all. Consider applying for extra time and other support, even for academically-able children; their diagnosis of ASC may mean they need this.

CHAPTER 6
Supporting sensory processing

Sensory information is sent to the brain through the senses, and the aspects of our sensory system enable us to experience, understand and respond to the world around us. Our sensory systems take in sensory information and send the messages to our brain where it is processed, and appropriate messages are sent to the body to react. We might do this consciously (e.g. responding to an invite heard over the phone) or unconsciously (e.g. immediately removing our hand away after touching a hot plate).

> It is cold outside. You look through the window and **see** the effects of the cold, such as frost on the lawn or clouds in the sky. You **feel** the cold on your skin as it raises goose bumps. You can **smell** and **taste** the cold in the air. You can **hear** the crunch of people's feet walking on frozen leaves. This information is processed by the brain, which then sends you an **action message**, such as 'Put your coat on, it's cold out there!'.

Sensory processing disorder (SPD) is a condition that affects many people, not just those with Autism Spectrum Condition (ASC). It can be common in people with Attention Deficit Hyperactivity Disorder (ADHD) and other conditions, but is also found in those with no co-existing condition. The DSM-5 diagnostic criteria now includes difficulties with sensory processing as part of ASC and therefore it is less likely to be diagnosed as a separate condition. However, it is a positive move that sensory processing difficulties should now be looked for and assessed when diagnosing children for ASC.

Many children with ASC have difficulty organising and regulating their sensory systems. It can be that sensory differences and difficulties are the major daily challenge for children with ASC. All the information we take in from and about the world around us dictates how we respond to changes in our own body, the environment and how we interact or respond to the situations and people we come into contact with. We take sensory information in via our ears, eyes, skin, mouth, nose and ears and this information is **integrated** by the brain. This is when it combines the sensory information (sounds, visions, smells, etc) into a coherent picture to tell us what is around us. For example, we see a plate of food, we smell a particular smell and feel that the plate is warm. Our brain makes sense of this information and tells us *'It's a bowl of chips, eat them.'* Our brains also **modulate** incoming sensory information to filter out unnecessary information (e.g. so we can ignore another plate of food on the counter that isn't ours). If the sensory system is easily overwhelmed and the brain finds it difficult to integrate and modulate all the sensory information around us, then every part of the day can become a major challenge; people are often in a noisy, busy, demanding and overwhelming environment for most of every day.

A child with sensory differences will likely have them for life. They can be regulated and sometimes change as children mature, but generally these differences will stay with them to some degree into adulthood.

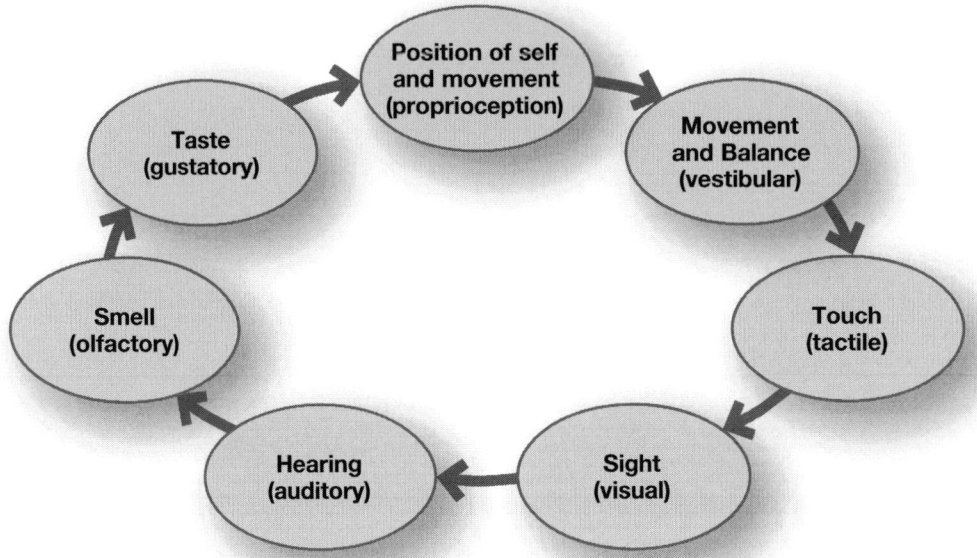

The seven aspects of the sensory system

In many children and adults with ASC, their sensory processing is affected in one or both of two ways:

1   Sensory dysregulation

This is when someone is unable to filter and process sensory information efficiently. This can lead to them being **hypersensitive** (over-sensitive), which can lead to sensory-avoiding behaviours or **hyposensitive** (under-sensitive), which can lead to sensory-seeking behaviours, to one or more (or indeed, all) of their senses. This makes the world seem like either 'too much' or 'not enough', and can lead to individuals being unresponsive to, avoiding or seeking out sensory experiences to try and regulate the input to their brain.

Sensory-avoiding behaviours commonly seen in children with sensory difficulties include:

➤ putting hands over their ears
➤ refusing to go into a room
➤ walking the long way round to something
➤ shouting
➤ screaming
➤ withdrawal from or not engaging with activities
➤ absenteeism.

Sensory-seeking behaviours commonly seen in children with sensory difficulties include:

➤ fidgeting
➤ the inability to sit still
➤ constant or obsessive chewing

➤ fiddling with a toy or something like Blu-Tack™

➤ pushing or hitting others

➤ extreme need to climb or seek out high places

➤ running away or twirling in circles at speed

➤ smelling or licking things

2　Sensory overload

Sensory overload is when the brain cannot filter out unnecessary sensory information, which becomes overwhelming, highly distracting, distressing or even painful. If noise, bustle, movement, verbal demands, smells and other sensory information become overwhelming for children with ASC, they could have a sensory meltdown (when they are often physically fighting to escape the source of distress) or shutdown (when they seem extremely quiet and unresponsive). This is when the brain is so overloaded that it shuts down some or all of its conscious functions, causing the child to go into 'fight or flight' mode or complete withdrawal. It is like a computer crashing. All systems are temporarily suspended; for some children, this may mean that they can't hear you speak to them, or they are unable to communicate with anyone, or they are unable to see clearly. As with a computer, the brain needs time to recover and reboot in a quiet and undemanding place.

Sensory differences

We all have different sensory sensitivities. For example, some people get car sick easily, need to wear sunglasses on a bright day, or have a particularly strong or poor sense of smell. However, for some children with ASC, it may be the case that their sensory systems are working in a different way to what is typical, so it is important to understand these differences and make accommodation for them. The differences may be subtle or acute. Once we have identified them, it is reasonable to make environmental adaptations or allow a child to opt out of certain activities.

The sensory system

The tactile, vestibular and proprioceptive senses are the foundational senses as they provide the building blocks for the other four senses.

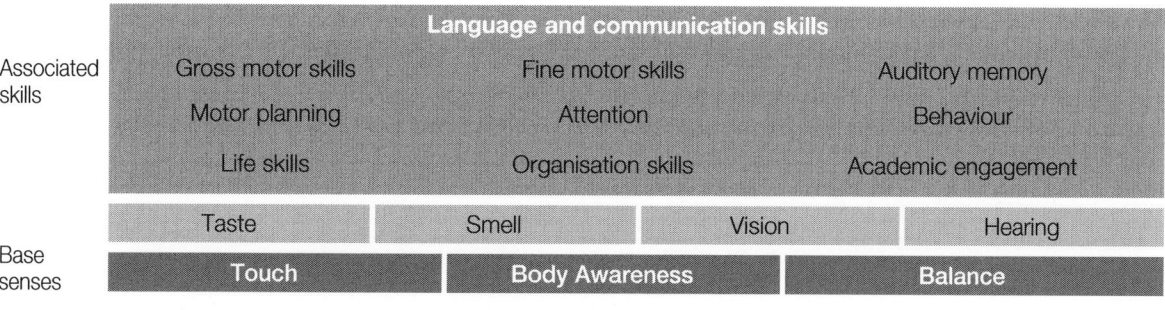

Sensory processing and how it affects other skills

Touch – the tactile system

The tactile system is responsible for our sense of touch. Our skin has receptor cells which send messages to the brain. It gives us information about pressure, temperature, light or firm touch, pain and vibration. The development of this system provides the building blocks for body awareness and motor planning, and it affects fine motor skills (e.g. the ability to put the correct pressure on a pencil in order to write). A good tactile system enables everyday activities, such as dressing, washing, brushing teeth, brushing hair, picking things up and manipulating toys and equipment, to be carried out successfully.

Our sense of touch performs a **protective function** in alerting us to danger and triggering our brain to send out signals to react. Therefore, touching a hot plate makes us pull our hand away, or someone getting too close to us makes us move away. It also performs a **discrimination function**. We can feel the texture, shape and other qualities of an object through touch.

If a child is **over-responsive** to touch:

- their system is excessively sensitive to their touch receptors. They may be so overwhelmed by the touch sensations assaulting their brain that switching focus to any other sensory input can be difficult.
- they may have to wear clothes inside out to avoid the sensation of labels or seams.
- they may hate standing next to others in case they brush against them, and may put a lot of effort into avoiding certain people or textures.
- they may also avoid messy play or outdoor play.
- they may be aggressive when others come near them, try to control activities or be very anxious.
- they may put so much energy into avoiding touch input from the environment and other people that there is little energy left for learning and social interaction.

If a child is **under-responsive** to touch:

- they may not register when and where they are being touched and so seem unresponsive to something like a light tap on the shoulder. This can impair their body awareness and gross motor skills.
- they can seek out heavy pressure, craving the sensory input.
- they may touch everything, and may not register pain as quickly as others, so their sense of danger does not develop well.
- they may have difficulty determining the nature of a texture, and find it difficult to pick things up. This will impair their learning development as they will have little tactile memory to draw on for activities such as design technology planning, imaginative writing and predicting the outcomes of science experiments involving materials. (Yack, Aquilla & Sutton, 2002; Kranowitz, 2005; Ayres, 2005).

Balance – the vestibular system

The vestibular system is located in our inner ear and is responsible for the information we receive about the movement of our head and body, awareness of gravity and where we are in relation to the ground. It has a **discrimination function**, which tells us things like whether we are still or moving, going fast or slow, going straight or in circles, whether we are high up or low down, and whether people and objects are moving or still. This links with our vision as we assess what is going on around us, which is a very important skill as children learn to cross the road. It also has a **protective function**, which makes us able to keep ourselves balanced on a wobbly surface or know which way is up when we are underwater, for example. It is important in supporting all our other senses and actions. It supports our posture, and our ability to maintain balance, move, maintain different speeds, find rhythm, stay calm, and plan our actions. It helps a child sit still, move around school and do PE.

If a child is **over-responsive** to balance:

- ➤ they will seem cautious when moving around.
- ➤ they may refuse to take part in or struggle in PE and may feel motion sickness when moving quickly. They may refuse to climb or seem to shake when doing so because they have a great fear of heights. Even turning their head to look around or behind them may be something they rarely do.
- ➤ they will avoid outdoor play, bicycles, climbing, stairs and escalators, and want to have their feet firmly on the ground. They may communicate their distress through refusal to take part in certain activities, crying, withdrawal, or fight or flight behaviour because they are so fearful of the activity they are being asked to do.

If a child is **under-responsive** to balance:

- ➤ they will likely seek out movement at every opportunity and will seem to be hyperactive and unable to keep still.
- ➤ their central nervous system may need excessive amounts of input to stay alert and organised, and keeping still long enough to focus attention on the lesson may seem impossible for them. This can have a great impact on their learning and ability to concentrate long enough to engage with the lesson and complete a piece of work.
- ➤ at playtimes, they might seem to have no sense of danger and may take many risks in search of the sensory input they seek. As their actions may not be well planned, they may impact on others who happen to be in the way (Yack, Aquilla & Sutton, 2002; Kranowitz, 2005; Ayres, 2005).

Body awareness – the proprioceptive system

The proprioceptive system is the body's ability to sense movement within joints and joint position, which enables us to know where our limbs are in space without having to look. Proprioception is responsible for understanding where our limbs are in relation to other parts of the body and to the objects around us. The protective and discrimination functions of this system overlap with the vestibular system in particular. We need to develop a **body map** (i.e. an understanding of our body, what it looks like, its shape, size and proportions) to help us plan movements and learn actions that help us develop skills. For example, forming a letter or number consists of certain movements that, if we repeat them enough, are committed to our body map memory, so writing that letter becomes an act of regular movements that we don't need to think about. Proprioceptive or whole-body activities help stimulate the brain to be more alert, as well as being calming when we are stressed or overloaded. For example, we move or stretch to revive our concentration when we've been sitting still for a long time. Exercise can make us feel either alerted or calm our levels of stress.

In general, exercise is important for both physical and mental health. A number of studies have shown that vigorous exercise is one of the best treatments for depression. Exercise can reduce stress and anxiety as well as improve sleep, reaction time, and memory.

Stephen Edelson

Children are not prone to proprioceptive over-sensitivity, but some may be under-sensitive and find the sensory information that they receive difficult to process. If this is the case:

➤ Their gross and fine motor skills may be delayed, or they may seem clumsy and awkward in their movements.

➤ They may seek out touch and pressure by leaning on people when they are stood up, leaning against walls, hugging people and squeezing themselves into tight places.

➤ They can find manipulating toys and equipment difficult and seem to be heavy-handed, often breaking things or knocking things over.

➤ They may struggle with neat handwriting and place to much or too little pressure on the pencil.

➤ They may find it difficult to judge or manage the motor planning involved in life skills such as brushing their teeth, washing, drying themselves, getting dressed and doing chores, and can be clumsy when performing these tasks (Yack, Aquilla & Sutton, 2002; Kranowitz, 2005; Ayres, 2005).

Sight – the visual system

The visual system gives us sight, and is developed along with the tactile, balance and body awareness senses so that we make sense of what we see. (If you see an apple, you can imagine how to hold it, what it will feel like and how heavy it is.) The visual system also informs our taste, smell and hearing senses. (Imagine smelling, tasting and hearing the crunch of an apple just by looking at a picture of one. Sometimes your mouth waters in anticipation!) As with other sensory systems, sight has the **protective function** in that it alerts us to danger by enabling us to see things in the distance, recognise objects and situations that have similarities to other dangers we are aware of, and see other people's body language in order to guess their intentions towards us. Sight also has the **discrimination function** of enabling us to distinguish between colour, shape, size, depth, distance, form, and movement.

If a child is **over-responsive** to visual stimulation:

➤ They may react defensively to static visual sensations in the environment such as busy classroom displays, striped carpets, shiny surfaces and fluorescent lights.

➤ They may not be able to find their way around the classroom because they are receiving too much visual information, or be able to focus on the whiteboard or worksheet.

➤ Things dangling from the ceiling and people moving around them may cause confusion and distress.

➤ Playing, learning to read and write, doing physical activity and looking at a person's face can be difficult for these children.

If a child is under-responsive to visual stimuli:

- They may not seem able to focus on an object, person, activity or event. This is because these children's visual systems are not connecting adequately to their other sensory systems, meaning their brains cannot put incoming information together as a whole picture.
- Matching shapes or pictures may be difficult, as will responding to look at the person who is talking to them even if they are listening clearly.
- They may seek out more visual stimulation by being very close to computer or TV screens and watching spinning or dazzling patterns on toys, screens and in the sunlight (Kranowitz, 2005).

Hearing – the auditory system

The auditory system enables us to hear and process sounds. It is important for children learning to speak and communicate, as they listen to the speech sounds around them and learn to imitate those sounds to speak themselves. Its **protective function** is to warn us of oncoming danger, such as traffic or the sound of something whizzing through the air towards us. In these instances, it informs our body movements and balance so that we can either move away or cover our ears. Its **discrimination function** enables us to develop the ability to listen, through hearing the quality, tone, volume, duration, and pace of a sound. We can learn to identify situations, objects and people by their sound. Listening skills are vital in the classroom to enable children to listen to the teacher, follow instructions and have conversations with others.

If a child is **over-responsive** to sound:

- They are often overwhelmed by the volume and intensity of sounds in the environment that others are able to filter out. Every scrape of a chair, tap of a pencil, tap of a keyboard or sniff can seem mega-loud to a child with this difficulty, and they will often put their hands over their ears.
- It can be painful, exhausting and extremely stressful for them to be in any environment that isn't silent (such as a school).
- It can affect their auditory discrimination skills and their ability to speak, use language socially, and access learning or other activities.
- Some rooms or environments (such as a toilet block) will feel insufferable and they may refuse to go to certain places as the noise will be too much for them.

If a child is under-responsive to hearing:

- They may seem to be deaf, not responding to certain sounds (especially quiet or soft sounds). However, a deaf child cannot hear, whereas auditory hyposensitivity is a difficulty with registering and responding to the sounds that are heard.
- They may not answer to their name or engage in conversation with others if they are not registering what the conversation is about. This is often because the brain is not modulating the separate sounds in the environment to register as speech directed at the child.
- It is usual to have their hearing tested, and also an auditory processing test may be done by an educational psychologist. However, also be aware that a child may just not want to respond rather than be unable to do so.

Taste and smell – the gustatory system

The senses of taste and smell are closely connected, as are all our senses. Their **protective function** is to warn us of dangerous foods or environmental dangers such as sour milk or dangerous gasses. Their **discrimination function** enables us to develop the ability to discriminate between many different flavour combinations and identify a food that is familiar to us just by its taste and smell.

> ► Children who are **over-responsive** to taste and smell may have a very limited diet and only eat certain foods.
>
> ► They may dislike any foods mixing on the plate, and either refuse to try new foods or gag when doing so.
>
> ► Putting things in their mouth or general smells around school and the wider environment may be very stressful for them.
>
> ► Lunchtimes in school, playgrounds (with their environmental smells such as children's snacks, traffic fumes or dog mess on nearby pavements) and teachers wearing perfume can be particularly difficult for them to deal with.
>
> ► Children who are **under-responsive** to taste and smell may not respond to strong smells and may seek to sniff people's clothes and hair in order to identify or feel comfortable with them.
>
> ► They may also be unaware of personal hygiene, especially when puberty is beginning (Kranowitz, 2005).

Identifying a child's sensory needs

When teaching and supporting a child with ASC, it is helpful to spend some time observing their behaviour and recording their sensory responses. These can be the simplest and seemingly unusual things that they avoid or seek out. Ask the child to say what things annoy them or attract them if they are able.

Ideally, an occupational therapist (OT) who is qualified in Sensory Integration should do a full assessment and put a sensory programme in place for children who need it. However, these therapists are few and funding is not readily available for assessments. If your area has this available, then it is a great resource. Some parents may pay for a private Sensory Integration Therapy assessment, which can be used in school, and sometimes includes training for staff, which schools may pay for.

Although teachers are not qualified to assess and implement therapy, they can learn enough to understand a child's sensory difficulties and implement calming or alerting activities that can make a real difference to their access to learning and self-regulation. This must be done in partnership with parents. Ideally, an autism specialist teacher should be consulted if you cannot access an OT qualified as a Sensory Integration Therapist. These can be sourced through the local authority, the National Autistic Society or recommendations from other schools.

Begin by reading about Sensory Integration Therapy. This is generally the main therapy to support sensory difficulties for children with ASC. However, there are general activities that can be done without having a full therapy programme in place and a specialist autism teacher should be able to advise you on this. Three particularly helpful books are *The out-of-sync child* by Stock Kranowitz, *Building bridges through sensory integration* by Yack & Aquilla, and *Sensory integration and the child* by Ayres & Robbins.

Providing a sensory diet

A sensory diet is a planned and scheduled activity program designed to meet a child's specific sensory needs.

Yack, Aquilla & Sutton, 2005

It is important to understand that a child may present with many challenging behaviours because they are having sensory difficulties. Sensory activities throughout the day can prevent these behaviours. A sensory diet is a series of regular sensory activities that meet a child's sensory needs in an appropriate way. The aim is to meet the child's sensory needs in a way that is comfortable, calming and appropriate. For example, a child who chews their jumper or fingers all the time may be given a chewy necklace (specifically designed for the purpose) instead.

Having sensory activities throughout the day can help a child with ASC organise their sensory system better and know what makes them feel calmer or more alert. This takes a lot of support at first but, as the child goes through the school, they can learn what works for them and know that they have access to appropriate activities.

All children with ASC should be taught about their sensory systems and how they can make themselves feel better. Sensory activities they can use will need to be individualised and monitored to make sure that they are helping the child as intended. Teachers and parents should not automatically assume what will work and how the child will respond. Involve the child in making choices and ask them to say or indicate what they like and don't like, and try all kinds of things. Sometimes a simple but creative idea can make all the difference.

A Sensory Integration Therapist may have regular sessions with a child to do more complex and specialised therapies. However, this chapter gives teachers of children with ASC some guidelines on how to include and schedule regular sensory activities for individual children in order to help them regulate themselves (i.e. become or stay calm or alert), so that they can be ready for learning and avoid becoming overloaded and distressed.

Case study

Dawn (Y2 pupil) had always found writing difficult. She was becoming more and more distressed and started to refuse to write altogether, saying that the paper was too 'strange' to touch. Juliet, her teaching assistant, asked Dawn to show her what paper she did like and Dawn showed her a laminated board book. Juliet laminated a piece of lined paper and now Dawn does all her writing on that. Each piece of work she does on it is photocopied to be put in her book.

A sensory diet can include:

- A box of sensory toys and objects that the child enjoys and finds calming, available for them to request whenever they need it.
- Sensory activities regularly timetabled throughout the day, inside or outside the classroom, so that the child knows what they will be doing and when. The child should be able to make choices and manage their sensory activities through being given choices and being able to access their sensory activities when they feel that they need them. Sensory activities should not be used as a reward for good behaviour;

we do not want the child to learn that they must be good in order to feel calm, as the activities that calm them help their behaviour. They need free access to them whenever possible.

➤ Whole-class activities matched to the child's sensory needs, such as vigorous exercise in a PE lesson or sensory experiences at storytelling time.

➤ 'Time out' or 'quiet time' with no sensory input or other demands.

➤ Specific sensory therapy activities carried out under the direction of an OT. These may include sensory exercises such as those a physiotherapist might prescribe, or specialist equipment such as white noise hearing aids.

How to create a sensory diet

The easiest way to begin is to first identify a child's sensory profile by filling in a questionnaire from a sensory therapist/OT. This will ask lots of questions about a child's responses to different sensory stimuli and will ask whether they do not respond to, seek out or avoid those stimuli. A variety of sensory resources can be collected and put in a box for the child to be available on request or when timetabled. The box can be added to the child's visual timetable as often as is necessary. A child may need to start the day with a sensory activity and have a sensory break between every class or learning activity. It is important to look at the child's school day to see where they are most in need of a break, and add in a sensory activity before they become overloaded or upset. It is also important to take heed of parents who identify that their child is having a meltdown when they get home from school.

> *There are many children with ASC who manage to keep everything under control throughout the school day and then all the tension explodes from them when they get home. This is like having a bottle of fizzy drink which is shaken throughout the day as each demanding situation is faced by the child. When they go home, the top is released and the fizz spills out in a massive and uncontrollable burst.*

If a child has this problem, then sensory activities throughout the day and at the end of the day will go some way to help them, so that their tension can be released gradually throughout the day. Sensory support can be offered by:

➤ **Minimising the sensory triggers** in the environment and learning activities (e.g. taking things that hang from the ceiling in the classroom down, putting blinds on the window, cutting labels out of clothing, slowing down the demands of instructions so the child has time to process what they are being asked to do)

➤ Giving the child an **activity that calms or alerts** their senses so that they are able to regulate themselves to a state where they are able to focus and engage with other activities and with learning in the classroom

➤ Using sensory activity to **desensitise the child to sensory overload** and enable them to access activities and places they could not previously. This kind of activity is usually covered in specific therapy. In school, it can mean that you are able to introduce a child gradually to something that they might otherwise refuse to do.

> ## Case study
>
> Malachi (Y4 pupil) was over-sensitive to sound and didn't like cold temperatures on his feet or body, which meant he hated PE. When it was time to go swimming, he was taken to the swimming pool on three separate occasions before the swimming lessons commenced, each time going further into the building. This was supported with a social story about what would happen when he went swimming with school. He was able to adjust himself to the sights, sounds and smells that he didn't like and was eventually able to tolerate and enjoy his swimming lesson.

Sensory Support Activities

Below are some ideas for sensory activities for each sensory area. This is a guide only and you will need to work with the pupil and their parents to find out what works for them. Never insist on them trying something that makes them distressed or overexcites them so much that they cannot calm down.

Aim to teach the pupil:

➤ that they can meet their need to seek out a sensory experience in an appropriate way
➤ to understand that they can organise their body and mind to be better at concentrating and learning
➤ to be able to calm themselves in anxious situations
➤ that it is okay to remove themselves from a painful or overwhelming sensory situation.

Sometimes pupils' sensory systems react so strongly to a situation that they are quickly overwhelmed and cannot prevent a sensory meltdown. Teachers will need to be aware that this can happen, and provide a safe and quiet recovery place if it is likely to happen.

Calming and organising sensory activities

If a child is over-responsive or sensory-avoiding they may need activities that calm their system so that they can manage the overload and understand how to self-regulate their sensory needs. **See CD-ROM for a sensory monitoring sheet template** to use alongside these activities.

Touch

➤ If the pupil is very touch-sensitive, the teacher should make whatever accommodation is needed to make the pupil comfortable and teach other pupils to give them space. Remember that they can feel extreme pain even at gentle touch. Teach others to stop touching the pupil (e.g. when passing them, in games, to get their attention, when sitting next to them) if the pupil tells them to.
➤ Consider PE clothing adaptations, such as wearing long jogging pants instead of shorts, to decrease the likelihood of a pupil being touched.
➤ Warn the pupil when you are going to touch them and ask them if it is okay. Approach from the front whenever possible. Teach others to do this too.

➤ Try different seating arrangements. A soft cushion or furry throw may make a chair more tolerable. Try a beanbag to sit on at carpet time.

➤ Give the pupil something soft or firm to squeeze or wrap themselves in (e.g. a stretchy fabric.) Firm, deep pressure is generally calming.

➤ The pupil can help put together a texture box of different fabrics or materials that they find calming.

➤ Show pupils how they can wash their hands in still rather than running water.

Balance

➤ Allow the pupil to do physical and movement tasks slowly and in smaller steps.

➤ Rhythmic movements such as rocking, bouncing and swinging can be calming. Wobble cushions on chairs or yoga balls can help some pupils.

➤ Have daily (or at least regular) one-to-one activity time on PE equipment so the pupil has the chance to develop their balance and co-ordination, and be more confident when they come across these activities in PE lessons.

➤ Encourage and support the pupil to enjoy after-school activities that develop balance (e.g. dance, karate) if they can tolerate this.

➤ Develop left and right co-ordination through labelling their hands or areas in a room *L* and *R*, practise finding and moving to left and right, and regular fine motor activities such as threading, cutting and using different writing implements (e.g. try using alternative writing tools like felt pens which need less pressure than a pencil).

➤ Put tape on the floor to help the pupil see where to go, where to stand and where to sit on the carpet.

Body awareness

➤ Rolling the whole-body on a body or yoga ball can be calming, as well as sitting in a rocking chair or on a beanbag. Generally, yoga can be very helpful in teaching body awareness.

➤ Encourage pupils to watch their movements in front of a mirror.

➤ Using playdough, Blu-Tack™, or fidget toys can help calm and organise a pupil's system while they are working, or for a time before work to alert their system.

➤ Arrange classroom furniture so the pupil can see the route from one place to another and travel it without having to squeeze past others or navigate obstacles (if at all possible!).

➤ Using a weighted toy, carrying a box of books from one class to another or wearing a backpack with a few books in it can help calm the proprioceptive system but should not be used all the time in order to protect the child's back. This is a good activity to add to a visual timetable.

Sight

➤ Make the environment less visually overwhelming if possible (see Chapter 2).

➤ Provide a dark tent or covered corner of the classroom so the pupil can hide away from visual stimuli.

➤ Use pictures on containers and label drawers to help the pupil know where to find things.

➤ Use a different coloured paper for worksheets, working with the pupil to discover which suits them best.

➤ Have a clear space all around the whiteboard, and plain muted walls where the pupil sits (on the carpet and at their table).

➤ Some pupils may find that turning to the wall or using a privacy screen helps them focus better on a work task as they shut out visual stimulation.

➤ Toys that gently move in waves or slow, constant movements can be visually calming, as can watching running water, bubble tubes and following the path of bubbles blown into the air.

Hearing

➤ Use clear and minimal words for giving instructions (see Chapter 3).

➤ Allow the pupil to wear headphones in very noisy environments, giving them the choice of when not to wear them (this shouldn't be all the time so that they learn that some environments are quiet and okay).

➤ Encourage a quieter classroom for all pupils.

➤ Minimise outside noise from open windows and turn off electrical equipment when it is not being used.

➤ Listening to music can be calming for some pupils.

➤ Provide warning of when noises might happen and what the pupil can do to stay calm when they do (e.g. provide a social story about what to do when the fire alarm goes off, and let them know when the drill will take place).

➤ Introduce a pupil to a new environment slowly so that they desensitise in their own time (e.g. take them to the swimming pool before they go swimming for the first time).

Taste

➤ Allow the pupil regular snacks of foods they will eat and introduce other foods of similar textures. Be mindful of their health and work with parents and specialists if they have major food intolerances.

➤ Separate the pupil's foods on a plate. Provide a visual schedule for lunch box so they can choose the order to eat their food. It can encourage a slow eater to eat quicker and to eat more varied items.

➤ A pupil who bites things or chews a lot might use a special chew toy, made from safe plastic for this purpose.

Smell

➤ Staff should ideally wear unscented deodorants and avoid wearing perfume or cologne.

➤ It may be necessary for alternative lunch arrangements to be made if the pupil cannot stand the food smell in the dining hall.

➤ Some pupils like scented candles, baby lotion, and soaps with calming scents such as lavender, flowers, vanilla and chocolate.

➤ It may be possible to use fewer scented cleaning products in the classroom.

Alerting sensory activities

If a child is under-responsive or sensory-seeking they may need activities that alert their sensory system so that they can develop focus and concentration, as well as understand how to self-regulate their sensory needs.

Touch

➤ Have lots of tactile activities available in a box for the pupil to play with.

➤ Deep pressure massage of hands, feet and back can be enjoyed by some pupils. Light touch (such as tickles running up an arm) can also be alerting.

➤ Fidget toys can distract a pupil from touching others when it's inappropriate to do so.

Balance

➤ Bouncing, swinging, spinning, climbing and rocking activities alert the sensory system. Never make them do something, but allow them to try and to choose which activities they do.

➤ Tie a band of elastic or stretchy material tied around the front legs of a chair for the pupil to bounce their legs against.

➤ Instigate a walk out of class or a run around the playground between lessons, not only at playtimes.

➤ Create physical jobs for the pupil to do (e.g. put up or take down chairs, carry books to another classroom, sweep the floor).

Body awareness

➤ Most types of physical exercise will alert the proprioceptive system. A pupil with ASC may be very agitated, fidgety in the morning and afternoon and need rigorous exercise to regulate their system and sensory needs.

➤ Encourage the pupil to use different parts of the body by rolling, crawling, jumping, climbing, using a body or yoga ball, bouncing, kicking, throwing and catching.

➤ Ask the pupil to pull or push against a wall, or roll large-wheeled objects from one place to another.

➤ Get the pupil to do silly animal walks that use different parts of the body (such as an elephant swinging his trunk or a snake slithering on the ground).

➤ Teach the pupil to follow actions in front of a mirror to help with their visual awareness of the body.

➤ Ask pupils to use stress balls, fidget toys and putty, or do exercises that build hand strength and hand–eye co-ordination.

➤ Give the pupil a space to go to if they need to pace or push on the wall in the middle of a lesson.

➤ Never take PE lessons or breaks away from a pupil.

➤ Teach about personal space and practise 'arm's length' space with all pupils.

➤ Use visuals to help the pupil identify areas of pain or discomfort on their bodies.

Sight

➤ Toys and moving objects can alert and stimulate sight. Bubbles, light toys, fibre optics, disco lights and shiny, colourful, spinning objects can be part of a sensory box.

➤ Different coloured paper can alert a pupil to a worksheet or piece of text they need to read. This is a good way to separate different parts of a task if it involves more than one sheet.

➤ Rather than ask the pupil to copy off the class whiteboard, let them copy off a whiteboard on their desk or give them a printed copy of the text and a highlighter to identify main points with.

➤ Use coloured felt tip pens to draw boxes around each part of a worksheet or set of written instructions to help the pupil see each step more clearly.

➤ Provide the pupil with lined paper instead of a blank piece of paper.

Hearing

➤ Speak to a speech and language therapist (SALT) about auditory processing activities (and ask if the pupil can be assessed for auditory processing disorder if this is a significant difficulty for them).

➤ Gain the pupil's attention by using their name first. See Chapter 3 for other communication strategies.

➤ Use visual supports for instructions, routines, self-help and work tasks.

➤ Play auditory discrimination games such as sound bingo. These may work listening to the sounds on headphones so that they can hear the sounds clearly and without background interference.

Taste

➤ Sucking on or biting ice cubes, chewing gum, drinking from a curly straw and using a battery-powered vibrating massager can stimulate the jaw.

➤ A blowing and sucking activity can alert the taste aspect of the sensory system. These kind of activities include blowing bubbles or feathers, blowing out candles, blowing up a football, musical whistles and learning to play a wind instrument or harmonica.

➤ A battery-powered toothbrush can also be used at school (before or after eating) to alert the system.

➤ Pupils can strengthen the tongue by exercising it (e.g. by sticking it out, up, side to side), curling it and licking lollipops and ice pops.

Smell

➤ Scented candles with strong and spicy smells can distract a pupil from inappropriate smells such as faeces which they can be drawn to. Alternatively, place a few drops of scented oil on a cotton wool ball and put in a plastic jar.

➤ Encourage pupils to eat strong-flavoured snacks.

➤ Use scented playdough. (This may need to be edible, depending on the pupil.)

➤ Use scented pencils, rubbers and toys.

CHAPTER 7
Developing independence and organisational skills

It is important right from the start to have high expectations of what a child with Autism Spectrum Condition (ASC) can achieve. A child in the Early Years may begin by needing a lot of adult support, but the aim should always be to provide them with the skills they need to do things for themselves, meaning they won't always need an adult to prompt them or do things for them. Therefore, independence and organisational skills need to be part of their Individual Education Plan (IEP) or specialist programme. All the strategies and resources in this book are aimed at promoting independence, whilst also teaching the child with ASC that there is support and help available to them during the journey to independence.

Using teaching assistants (TAs) effectively

Studies have shown that in some schools, TAs are the primary educators of children with SEND. Busy teachers often don't have the time to meet with specialist teachers, educational psychologists, speech and language therapists (SALTs) and other outside agencies; therefore, the TA is often the one leading programmes and interventions, and differentiating work for children with ASC.

Many TAs are highly experienced and qualified (some are ex-teachers), but there are also TAs who are new to the role and learning how to support a child with ASC. Some children with ASC have high levels of need that require high levels of support. If their behaviour is challenging, the TA can easily become discouraged and stressed by thinking that everyone expects them to deal with the behaviour alone.

Sharples, Webster & Blatchford (2014) urge school leaders and teachers to strongly consider these seven evidence-based recommendations:

1 Do not use TAs as substitute teachers for low-attaining children.
2 Use TAs to add value to what teachers do, not replace them.
3 Use TAs to help children develop independent study skills and manage their own learning.
4 Ensure TAs are fully prepared for their role in the classroom.
5 Use TAs to deliver high-quality one-to-one and small-group support using structured interventions.
6 Adopt evidence-based interventions to support TAs in their small group and one-to-one instruction.
7 Ensure explicit connections are made between learning from everyday classroom teaching and structured interventions.

Teachers and TAs can make a great team. Communication is a huge factor in establishing a working relationship in which each party is clear of their roles and responsibilities. This should be established at the beginning of the school year by sitting down and discussing how the partnership will work.

Often TAs are unclear about their responsibilities in planning and differentiating work, recording progress, setting targets and managing behaviour, and unsure of who to go to for help on a difficult day and whether they should work with other children or not. They often feel a great responsibility for the child they have been appointed to but having a TA stuck like VELCRO® to a child is not helpful for either of them.

If the TA is off sick or away on a course, the child may refuse to work with anyone else. The teacher can also become reliant on the TA to the point of hardly knowing the child with ASC themselves. The TA should become more like 'elastic' than 'VELCRO©', able to stretch away from the child at times, and spring back when they are needed.

These are some useful tips to consider at the very start of developing the role of the TA working with a child with ASC:

- The teacher and TA should seek training about ASC. Whole-school training is best, but courses that the two of them can attend together also work very well.
- The teacher should be teaching the child with ASC. They should know their abilities, support their learning and know what works best to engage them in learning.
- The teacher should be aware of the TA's knowledge and understanding of ASC, and their practical and creative skills. Listen to them and remember to praise and thank them.
- The TA needs to be given copies of the classroom planning and be asked if they have any suggestions as to how the child with ASC can be motivated and included, especially if it is a topic or subject they are usually not keen on.
- The teacher and TA need to plan regular meetings and timetable them in.
- If the TA needs to make resources such as visual timetables or write social stories, they need to be given time during their working hours to do so. Resource preparation time will pay off massively as the child will have all they need, and the TA will be ready and prepared. This also needs timetabling and valuing as part of the TA's work.
- Consistency is key. Any visuals that are being used need to be referred to by both the teacher and the TA. They should try not to contradict something that the other has said to the child. This is particularly important in behaviour support.
- Behaviour strategies should be agreed. It is useful to put them into a **behaviour support plan (see CD-ROM)** so that their consistency can be maintained.
- If a child cannot understand a task, the TA should be given licence to change or move on from the task. They should take time to discuss this with the teacher if the task needs to be done later or doesn't need doing at all because the child has done something more relevant for them, such as working on one of their Individual Education Plan (IEP) targets.
- If the TA needs to work with other children at times, a social story or visual support can be used to help the child with ASC get used to this. The same applies to the child working with other TAs or adults. The child should still have a planned and prepared way of getting help when they really need it.

➤ At times, the TA will need to communicate with the child when the teacher is talking. Visual symbols or a whiteboard to draw or write on will help prevent the need to talk over the teacher.

➤ The teacher and TA should work together to include the child with ASC in class lessons. Teachers can help by not talking for too long, and making sure the child has something to listen out for or an activity to keep them engaged. They should also support them to be involved in group activities where they can interact with other children.

➤ Sometimes TAs may need to withdraw the child for individual intervention work, such as speech and language and social skills work or sensory therapy. The teacher can organise other children to be involved in this alongside the child with ASC to give them support and encourage peer relationships. It is often the case that other children can have similar needs and will benefit from the interventions too.

➤ If interventions are carried out outside of class, a child with ASC may learn the skill in only one context and will need to learn the same skill in other contexts (including home if applicable). Teachers and TAs should work out a plan for how the child will generalise and use the skills learned within everyday classroom teaching and activities.

➤ The TA should be aiming to do themselves out of a job! They should be looking for opportunities for the child to become more independent over time, to be able to do things with less prompting and join in with their peers in regular class routines and activities. The extent to which this can be done depends very much on the child with ASC and their level of need, but remember to be 'elastic' and not VELCRO© to the child.

➤ Teachers and TAs should remember that everyone has a bad day occasionally. Be kind to one another and don't try to blame anyone if the child has a bad day. Don't take things personally and look at the situation as if you were an observer. Smile and laugh; it will keep you going. Remember, tomorrow is always a new day; teach the child this too.

Developing organisational and independence skills in children with ASC

Some children with ASC may have difficulty with executive functions, but by no means all. This is not a marker of a child's intelligence but can be a barrier to them accessing learning because of their poor organisational abilities. Executive functioning difficulties can include:

➤ planning (both mental planning and organising a plan on paper)

➤ decision-making (they are often overwhelmed by choice)

➤ imagining outcomes (this is important in coping with changes and new experiences)

➤ breaking down a task into steps towards the outcome

➤ timing and organising themselves to do something in a given time

➤ reviewing progress through self-monitoring

➤ Understanding that others may have different views and opinions

➤ Behaviour inhibition (i.e. difficulty holding back impulsive behaviours)

- Switching attention (e.g. between topics of conversations, transitions from one activity to another)
- Problem-solving
- What to do in certain situations (particularly if an immediate response is required)
- Risk assessment (this affects their awareness of danger)
- Sustaining attention on non-preferred activities
- Initiating communication

A child with ASC can have difficulty with these skills because of their communication, sensory, flexible thinking and social understanding differences. This can mean that instructions and the presentation of learning tasks makes them difficult to attempt without support. Supporting children's independence should be part of their personal learning plan.

Early Years

In the Early Years class, children with ASC have a lot to learn about how school works. It is best to focus on 'how to be at school' skills (such as where to go in the classroom and what to do when you get there, how to sit and listen, how to wait, how to line up, play skills, taking turns) and guide children through any everyday routines and tasks that you want them to be able to do. It is important to use visual supports and social stories so that the child understands exactly what to do, how to do it and has had enough practice to be able to do it in a reasonable amount of time. The type of skills that may need to be taught will vary from child to child but may include:

- feeding themselves
- toileting
- making choices about which activity to do
- lining up
- sitting on the carpet
- answering the register
- waiting
- taking turns
- sharing attention (e.g. looking at what others are doing or looking at what the teacher is drawing attention to)
- walking to a different place in the school, such as the hall or outside area
- putting their coat on
- playing with a wider range of toys
- knowing what to do if they are upset

Visual supports should be used to show a child with ASC that a task can be done in a sequence and what the steps of the sequence are. Begin with between one and two steps and extend them as the child is able. Backward-chaining (where the first two tasks are done by the adult and the child does the last step) is a good way to introduce the schedule. This is then reduced to one step done by the adult and the next two steps done by the child, and so on, until the child can do all the steps. A good source of visuals for organisation and routines can be found on the Do2Learn website – www.do.2learn.com.

Social stories (see Chapter 8) can be a very good resource to help a child understand why they are being asked to do something. They can be made into a series of short booklets about being at school. They work best when the child is able to contribute to the story (e.g. by taking or choosing accompanying pictures) and when it is positive and leads to a successful learning experience. Social stories can also be used for the whole class.

KS1

If a child with ASC is making good progress and learning to follow regular routines in their classroom and around school (even if some prompting is still needed), it is important to continue to develop their skills throughout Y1 and Y2. Organising and completing a piece of work using a workstation and other supports are covered in Chapter 5, but there are other skills that can be developed too. These may include:

- getting changed for PE
- putting their coat on and fastening it
- collecting equipment
- giving out equipment
- putting equipment away
- asking for help
- working with a partner on a shared task
- developing a longer attention span
- developing memory and recall skills.

Another good skill to teach is that of self-checking. A visual schedule is very useful as a self-checking tool as it is always there and can be accessed easily without an adult having to constantly repeat the instruction.

Remember that a child with ASC may have a longer processing time, so pausing and giving them time to work out what they need to do should be part of the support they are given. Cutting back on adult prompting can also encourage more spontaneous and natural peer interactions, especially when the child with ASC is able to show others what they need to do, or other children can help them. Again, backward-chaining can be a helpful way of introducing a skill and making it successful for the child. A successful child is much more motivated and willing to do activities and learn to do them independently.

Social stories can continue to be used to develop a child's skills and understanding of routines, such as lining up and why we have assemblies. A social story helps a child understand why they are doing an activity and who or what is there to help them, whereas a schedule simply shows the routine to follow.

Other strategies include:

- using a sand timer to show how long a session or activity will last
- showing photographs of the finished task (e.g. a tidy carpet area)
- adding photo labels to boxes so that children know where things should go
- giving positive reinforcements, specific praise and reward charts for attempting tasks.

KS2

The transition to KS2 can be a good opportunity to develop organisation and independence skills in children with ASC. Again, this will be dependent on the child's individual abilities and needs. Some children continue to need a high level of one-to-one support in KS2, but some are able to develop more independence and join in with most lessons and activities so that the TA can work with others.

There can be many challenges for a child with ASC and it is important to develop their skills without putting them under too much pressure. An already anxious child will be overwhelmed by even more demands and so new skills must be introduced gradually. The child may benefit more from practising their existing skills in different contexts, and being able to rest from those demands if necessary.

We must be aware in KS2, as in all Key Stages, that the child's anxiety and coping levels must be monitored closely. One of the most important independence skills they can learn is how to organise their day so that a calming sensory activity can be accessed when it is needed.

Visual timetables are still a good strategy to support organisation and independence skills at this stage, and may be given as lists if the child is a good reader. This is a good skill for upper KS2 children to learn. The practice of ticking things off on the list once they have been completed helps organisational skills and develops satisfaction for a job well done.

Home and school working together

When parents and school work together to support organisation and independence skills, children with ASC can benefit from many more opportunities to generalise and practise their skills.

Case study

Robert (Y2 pupil) was having trouble taking turns when playing and speaking, and was getting very frustrated and upset. The challenge was to teach him about waiting, and he was supported to play a game in which the presence of a yellow circle meant he had to wait. When the wait had finished, the yellow circle was removed. The waiting times were short to start with and worked well in school.

At home, Robert's parents used the yellow circle to help him learn to wait for his dinner, rather than raiding the cupboards for snacks. The same signal was used to indicate that he needed to wait for his turn on the games console when his brother was playing on it.

Robert's school and parents worked together, were consistent and positive and did not make waiting a punishment. Therefore, this strategy was successful and Robert experienced many positive consequences, such as better playtimes, because he could now wait for someone to finish with the equipment he wanted to play with.

Schools don't have the time to work on all the situations that may cause difficulties at home but if what is happening at school is affecting home and vice versa, for example sensory overload, then it is worth focusing on these with parents to see if some accommodation can be made or skill can be taught to help the child. Giving children with ASC jobs in the class and around school (e.g. giving out equipment or mentoring younger children) is a great way to build their working with others skills as long as the task is clear, structured and they know what their role is. Giving children with ASC some responsibility can help them build confidence and learn to be organised.

CHAPTER 8
Social stories™

Social stories are one of the strategies that can be used to support children with Autism Spectrum Condition (ASC) in primary schools. They can also be used by parents and by others in the community (e.g. scout leaders, swimming teachers, doctors, dentists). Teachers and teaching assistants (TAs) are often advised to use social stories to support the behaviour and social skills of children with ASC, but are sometimes left without the advice and support they need to actually write good, effective social stories.

What is a social story?

Social stories were invented by Carol Gray in the early 1990s. A social story is written for an individual and is a permanent, visual story that describes and explains a social situation, issue or skill that that individual finds difficult to understand.

The aim of a social story is to provide the social information that the child is missing or misunderstanding so that they can make informed and supported choices about how they are going to respond to a particular social situation in an appropriate way. They should also be positive, affirming and celebrate the child's abilities and achievements.

Social stories can cover almost any subject, from personal habits to dealing with a death in the family, from school events to world events. Social stories gives the child an explanation about the perspectives of others; their beliefs, opinions, common social conventions, likes and dislikes. They often explain why people do the things they do.

Case study

George (Y1 pupil) did not want to choose a book to read, telling his teachers that he wasn't interested in reading. However, his teachers realised that he also had difficulty in understanding the point of stories due to his very literal thinking. However, they wanted him to experience and enjoy books that were linked to his particular interest of animals. They wrote a social story to encourage him to start with reading books about animals and added pictures. Once they had harnessed his interest in animals and reduced the pressure on him to choose a storybook, they found that he began to choose information books (and later storybooks) with animals in them.

A social story should not be written because you want a child to change their behaviour (other strategies can be used for that), but to help them understand a situation better and so perhaps respond to it differently.

Gray, 2001

The structure and format of writing an effective social story should always be followed to ensure that the story will support and help the child, rather than overload them with information and instruction. Social stories can be written for any age, and should be presented in a way that is age- and developmentally-appropriate for the individual. They can be written by parents or anyone who works with the child, and can cover any setting, event or situation. Indeed, when a member of school staff or a parent is confident in writing positive and affirmative social stories, then staff and parents can work together to write social stories for situations at home and at school. They can plan what will go in the story together or actually write it together, if both feel confident to do so.

Before you begin

A social story cannot be written without first having an understanding of the child and how they perceive a particular situation. A child with autism will have a logical reason for reacting or responding in a certain way. It is always useful to consider the following questions and discover the best answers you can through talking to the child, observing them, asking parents for their perspective and thinking about how the child's ASC is impacting on their perspective of the situation. This will help you find out what needs to be taught or explained to them to form the basis of the social story.

Questions about the child

1 What are the child's strengths, talents and interests?
2 What is the child's reading ability?
3 How much information can they process in one section?
4 Does the child have any sensory processing issues that may be impacting on their response to the situation?
5 Does the child understand language literally?
6 What makes the child stressed?
7 What makes the child calm and happy?

Questions for the parents and adults working with the child

1 What do they think causes or triggers the child's response?
2 How do they usually react to the child's response to the situation?
3 What effect is their response having on the child's behaviour?
4 Do they have any strategies that usually help the child?

Questions about the context

1 What is happening?
2 Where is it happening?
3 When is it happening?
4 Who is it happening to and with?
5 How is it happening?

You can then try to draw some conclusions about why a situation is happening, taking into account all of the above information. Ensure you consider the child's autistic perspective: what seems logical to them?

> *Don't assume you and your pupil have the same social understanding. Don't forget to ask the child what they think and observe the situation carefully. Often what they are missing is something that is totally obvious to you.*

When considering the best way to present your social story, take account of:

- the child's reading ability
- their concentration span
- their specific interests
- how much information they might be able to process in one sitting.

If a child is a non-reader then the illustrations in a social story will be the main communication tool, and the text will be simple sentences that form a script for the adults presenting the story to the child, so that the language remains consistent regardless of who is reading it to the child.

Devise a goal and title

The main purpose of a social story is to give the child some social information that they are missing, or a better understanding of something they have misinterpreted. A social story may also reduce the child's stress and anxiety about an issue, situation or future event, or celebrate the child's achievements and reinforce their positive self-awareness. Social stories can also be written to prepare the child for a new experience and to help them understand a new concept (e.g. why people leave a space between themselves and others when they are talking). Those writing the story should also have in mind how they would like to help change how a child responds to a situation. It is important to remember to be positive, affirming and teaching. Often the negative behaviour a story is targeting is not mentioned, or it is explained so that the child understands why a different approach could be beneficial to them.

When you have decided on the purpose of the social story, draft a title. The title of a social story needs to explicitly say what the story is about and be literal. Remember that it is the first thing the child reads or hears, so it should also encourage them to want to read on.

Here are some example titles for social stories. The child needs to be able to tell what the story is about from the title.

- I can greet people I know
- There are toilets at the supermarket that I can go to
- People in my class like the models I make
- Growing up brings a lot of unknown things, but that's okay
- I am clever and accomplished

Writing the social story

Drafting a social story is a daunting process. Often, people write stories that are too wordy, unspecific or negative, which are ineffective. Occasionally, a misguided attempt at writing a social story can make a situation worse. Here is an example of something that is *not* a social story:

When playtimes are bad

When the children play out at our school we need to play gently and carefully so we do not hurt each other. The bigger children, like me, need to be extra careful not to be rough with the little children. You can often get carried away and get too rough with each other while playing. It is up to you bigger children to show the little ones how to behave because they do not always understand.

At playtime today, it went very badly. You hurt two children and they were VERY upset. If you keep on having bad playtimes, you will not be allowed to go out at all.

We all need to stop and think from time to time about our behaviour, and check ourselves to make sure we are not being too rough whilst playing.

What are your thoughts about this story?

- Is it positive or negative?
- Who is it blaming?
- Is the switch between first person and third person confusing?
- Is it suggesting solutions?
- Does it explain the situation accurately?
- Does the child have something positive and constructive to learn from this story?

A good social story is objective, positive, emotionally safe, encouraging and informative, and explains a situation in language that the child can understand. It has a clear structure. It explains the social perspective and leaves the child with positive suggestions about how they can deal with a situation more positively. It makes suggestions and gives choices. It does not usually use absolutes like 'must' or 'need to'.

This social story would have appropriate illustrations inserted into it and be presented to the child in an attractive format. Here is the above story written as a true social story.

Having a great playtime

My name is Rosy and I am in Y4 at Leafy Lane School.

We have a playtime in the morning and after we have eaten our lunch.

I like to play with the infant children at playtimes. It is good to have friends to play with. These are my friends in the infants.

The children in the infants are smaller than me. This is because they are younger and have not grown as tall as me yet.

I like to be a kind friend. I like to play nice games with my friends.

Sometimes I might bump into one of my friends or hold them tightly when we are playing together.

People don't like it if they are held tightly or when someone bumps into them. They might fall or cry because they are hurt.

I can try to stop before I bump into someone.

I can try to hold someone gently when we are playing together.

This will make everyone happy and we can have good playtimes. Well done me and my friends!

Let's look at how it is structured in more detail. It is helpful when writing a social story to think in terms of a story structure – a beginning, middle and an end.

Beginning

The beginning of the story is where you set the scene and draw the child in. It is personal to the child and describes a situation or event literally and objectively. It clearly identifies the topic of the story, as stated in the title, and affirms and encourages the child from the outset. It is usually written in the present tense. It is written in first person narrative and takes account of how the child would speak of themselves. In Rosy's situation, for example, the staff might have discovered that Rosy is finding it hard to understand appropriate touch, doesn't have many ideas for games and is just a bit uncoordinated.

> **Having a great playtime**
>
> My name is Rosy and I am in Y4 at Leafy Lane School.
>
> We have a playtime in the morning and after we have eaten our lunch.
>
> I like to play with the infant children at playtimes. It is good to have friends to play with. These are my friends in the infants:

This text is reassuring, celebrates Rosy's strengths and helps her understand the exact situation the story will talk about. The 'wh' questions *what, where, who* and *when* have also been answered.

These are the **descriptive sentences** that Gray (2001) describes.

The middle

This is where we introduce the **perspective sentences** that will help explain the social information that we wish to help the child understand and enable them to explore how they feel about it (Gray, 2001). We should be careful to stay positive and make sure we do not put blame on the child for something they have done in response to a situation. We are aiming to help the child understand why things happen the way they do and what other people might be thinking, believing and doing. In this case, the younger children's perspective is given.

> The children in the infants are smaller than me. This is because they are younger and have not grown as tall as me yet.
>
> People don't like it if they are held tightly or when someone bumps into them. They might fall or cry because they are hurt.

The ending

The end of the story summarises the situation and makes suggestions as to what the child could do differently and what support is available, and reassures them that they are not in trouble. These **directive sentences** help the child understand what positive actions they could do now. It is important that the social story is balanced with more describing and explaining than directing. Gray (2001) suggests that for every five descriptive or perspective sentences there should be no more than two directive sentences. This is where the story suggests the positive behaviours that the child could adopt to make the situation work for them and others. It is important to be careful of the words used in suggesting possible actions to the child. Nothing should be absolute, so resist using words such as *must, will* or *should* and instead use *can, could* or *try*. You could explain what support is available, and for some children it might be helpful to state what rewards they will receive (e.g. they might be able to do a favourite activity). It can be useful for some children to make the last line a repeat of the title, to link everything together.

> I can try to stop before I bump into someone.
>
> I can try to hold someone gently when we are playing together.
>
> This will make everyone happy and we can have good playtimes. Well done me and my friends!

Other types of sentences

Affirmation sentences should be placed throughout the story to reassure and affirm the child. They offer a break from the main content and help the adult writing the story remember that they need to be positive and celebrate the child's gifts, abilities and achievements.

Partial sentences are there to enable the child to contribute to the story. They can be questions to be answered or sentences to complete (e.g. *'The things I like to do at school are…'*).

Co-operative sentences state how others can help the child and are often part of the directive sentences (e.g. *'My teaching assistant can help me by giving me my choice board.'*) (Gray, 2015).

This social story has not mentioned bad behaviour, getting angry or being stressed. Often the issue people think needs to be addressed isn't the one that needs to be written about in the social story at all.

See CD-ROM for an activity on structuring a social story that can be done individually or, even better, with others. See if you can identify the **descriptive**, **perspective** and **directive sentences** in each story. There are also **affirmation sentences** to help keep the story reassuring and positive and provide natural pauses in the text.

Review and illustrate

It is really important to read the social story you have written and check that it is going to do what you intend for the child. You need to check that it has a patient and encouraging tone and is literally accurate (and if literally interpreted, will not lead to unintended consequences). A useful checklist for writing social stories can be found on the Carol Gray Social Stories website, www.carolgraysocialstories.com, click on the Social Stories tab then 'What is a social story?'.

Then, you are ready to type or write out the story and add illustrations. Illustrations are a crucial part of putting the story together for the child. They are there to enhance the meaning of the story, and help children to process the language and ideas you are presenting to them. Illustrations also enable you to separate the text into chunks that the child can process. You can use images found online, photos of the child or setting, symbols or the child's drawings. Take time to think about what the pictures are communicating and keep them simple. For example, they can illustrate the child's favourite interests or characters to help them know that the story is positive and relevant to them.

Present your story to the child

Once you have your story prepared and have checked it, you can then present it to the child with ASC. You may want to laminate it for longevity but this is not usually necessary unless the child likes to tear paper. Print more than one copy so that you have a spare and can send a copy home for parents to keep and read with their child at home.

Top tips

- ▶ Think about where and when you will share the story with the child, and try to choose a calm and relaxed time and place with minimal distractions.
- ▶ The child may want to read the story to themselves or you can read it to them (particularly the first time).
- ▶ It is important to read it slowly. Allow time for the child to process the language and for them to respond if they so wish.
- ▶ Speak in a patient, calm and positive tone.
- ▶ Once the story has been read, you can ask the child what they think about it or explain the activities you are going to do to support them.
- ▶ Keep the story somewhere the child can access.

The story usually needs reading a few times to the child over the first weeks after it is introduced, and by different people. The social story is not a tool for nagging the child, but should offer them positive encouragement and help in a situation they find difficult. The frequency with which you read it with the child needs to be right for them. Some children love to keep their stories themselves and refer to them when they need to. Others get fed up of the story after a while but this is often because they have moved on and have been able to deal with the issue confidently.

If the child has a negative reaction to the story, becomes upset or refuses to read it, it is best to put it aside and review whether the content is suitable, the tone used to read it was demanding or negative, or that the story just wasn't explaining the right issue. Social stories can be difficult to master but once they begin to be a positive support for a child, they can provide a helpful toolkit of information that will help the child with ASC develop their social understanding, negotiate anxious situations and new experiences, and learn new skills. They can be a positive source of affirmation, and a celebration of the talents and progress that the child is making at school and home.

CHAPTER 9
Behaviour support

Behaviour in ways that others identify as 'challenging' or problematic is not exclusive to people with autism. It is part of being human. Most of our behaviours reflect attempts to meet our needs, satisfy our desires, cope with frustrations and high levels of emotion.

Clements & Zarkowska, 2000

Children with Autism Spectrum Condition (ASC) can have the same variety of behaviours as all children in a primary school. Some follow all the rules, are keen to please the teacher and have impeccable manners. Others may seem to be engaged in low-level disruptive behaviours, which annoy and distract teachers and other children. Some engage in repetitive behaviours that are self-stimulating but are seen as odd or annoying by others. Some display destructive, obstinate, challenging and harmful behaviours that impact on themselves and others, disrupting everyone's learning.

Try to understand any disruptive or challenging behaviours from the viewpoint of a child with ASC. It is also important to understand that their behaviours need to be 'read' correctly. Teachers need to be asking what the behaviour is communicating rather than immediately assuming that the child is being 'naughty' or 'doing it on purpose'.

Try not to take a child's behaviour personally, and look at working with the child to develop appropriate behaviours.

Many experts on ASC and behaviour explain that the behaviour we see is only the visible demonstration of underlying issues and conditions. Cumine et al. (2009) explain this as 'the iceberg of behaviour': what we see above the surface is only a fraction of the mass underneath the surface that we have to understand in order to adapt and change behaviours.

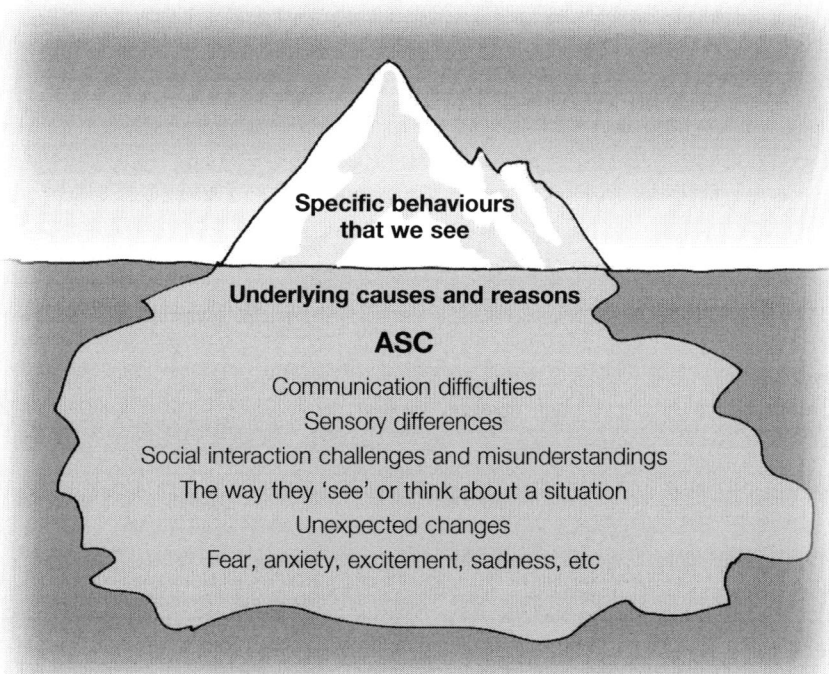

**Specific behaviours
that we see**

Underlying causes and reasons

ASC

Communication difficulties

Sensory differences

Social interaction challenges and misunderstandings

The way they 'see' or think about a situation

Unexpected changes

Fear, anxiety, excitement, sadness, etc

The iceberg of behaviour for children with ASC

> *Remember that children with ASC who manage to 'keep it all together' at school all day often have daily meltdowns or shutdowns as soon as they get home. Having good behaviour at school does not necessarily mean the child does not have significant challenges because of their ASC throughout every school day.*

ASC is a condition affecting communication, social understanding, sensory regulation and flexible thinking. Therefore, a child's inappropriate and challenging behaviour could be for any number of reasons and is often linked to high levels of stress and anxiety. The issue for many teachers is that it can display in the classroom as wilful disobedience and distraction. The child may not engage in activities or get on with their work. They may make constant noises, call out, talk over others or become distressed and argumentative. They may sit too close to others, be unable to share and play with others, work in a group, take things that are not theirs, not follow instructions, bang their head on the table, fiddle with something or be unable to sit still. They may become very angry, hit out at others, throw things, shout and scream, hurt themselves, or destroy equipment. They may refuse to move, run away, threaten others, or throw things. They may interrupt, and always say what they think. They may think they know more than the teacher and say so. They may refuse to do writing tasks, or not start or complete a piece of work without constant prompting. They may panic about change, or refuse to go in the hall because it smells different or they can't sit in their usual seat. They may cry, wet themselves or become completely withdrawn.

> *Any child can exhibit any behaviour if circumstances lead them to it. A child with ASC is no different. It is the challenges that children face which make them stressed and anxious, which they may sometimes communicate through 'challenging' behaviours.*

It is clear, then, that children with ASC need a supported approach to their behaviour. The first question we should always ask is '*What is making them anxious?*', then '*What is it that they don't understand?*'.

Taking the time to observe and investigate the function of the child's behaviour can be the most effective way to begin to understand the child and reduce stress for them, and support positive and appropriate behaviours.

Your school may have a behaviour monitoring system that can be utilised or you can use something like a STAR (Setting, Triggers, Actions, Results) record which is quick to complete and can be useful in gathering information (**see CD-ROM for a STAR record template**). If a child is verbal, don't forget to ask the child about their behaviour. It isn't just asking them to explain themselves, as many won't be able to; it is about asking them about the people, the environment, their perceptions and what they think are the triggers. It can be difficult for some children to express their thoughts, but others may welcome the opportunity to talk about their anxieties.

If a child is non-verbal or unable to explain the reasons behind their behaviour (which is very common even in very able children with ASC), then it is up to the teaching staff and parents to observe them in their environment. They need to see if there are any obvious triggers that might identify what the child is trying to achieve from their behaviour (see below for more information). However, remember that memories, sensory overload and internal emotional states not related to anything immediately obvious in the environment can also trigger a child's anxiety and behaviour.

Early Years

Children with ASC face many challenges as they start school from the environment, demands and social interactions. If there is understanding of their condition and strategies to support their needs, then supporting appropriate behaviour will be part of those strategies. They may not be able to communicate when something is overwhelming or they don't understand what you are asking of them. They may not know what to do in situations that other children can navigate easily and can be socially disadvantaged or excluded because of their differences. We have said that behaviour is a form of communication. It is also an instinctive reaction to frustration, fear and anxiety. A child's behaviour can seem inappropriate but it is telling you that there is something wrong or something they cannot cope with.

Be aware that a child with ASC may not understand why you are asking them to do something. Social stories or visual timetables can help them learn how to navigate and do what is expected of them in the school routine and learning activities.

When a child with ASC behaves in a way that prevents them or others from accessing learning, question whether the learning activity is accessible to the child. Do they know:

> - what they are supposed to be doing?
> - how they should be doing the activity? (i.e. how do they begin, what do they do next and how can they modify the activity to provide a variety of outcomes? Even playing with trains or other toys can be supported in this way)
> - how long they have to do the activity?
> - what support is available for them to achieve the activity?

Then identify how you can teach appropriate behaviour through demonstration, visual support and (if necessary) rewards. Success breeds success; many strategies, such as clear verbal communication and visual support, can help a child with ASC succeed in doing what they need to do in the classroom.

Motivating a reluctant child

Many children develop **intrinsic motivation**; they want to please their teacher, they like learning and being successful at a task, they get pleasure out of doing things along with their peers and want to be seen as a 'good' child. But intrinsic motivation can be too abstract for a child with ASC because it relies on being aware of wanting to please others, doing things for the good of a group or more abstract reasons. This can take much longer to develop in those with ASC. They may also struggle to understand the point of doing an activity; maybe they've done it before, they already know how to do it, they feel they can't do it, or they are just not interested.

Extrinsic motivation in the form of a visual chart or tangible reward can help, if matched correctly to the child's interests. Many children with ASC do not like doing something they think they've already done, but teachers need them to practise a skill and learn to generalise it. Tasks can become based on their particular interests. For example, if their interest is ponies, a pony jigsaw could be made to help the child 'earn' pony pieces each time they have attempted an activity. Making this successful is important and jigsaw pieces earned should not be taken away once given. Whatever strategies you use to motivate the child need to be successful and not provide them with another form of stress.

KS1

If a child with ASC begins to be more confident and able to follow classroom routines and behaviour expectations, but perhaps has some habits that are disrupting their learning (e.g. calling out, complaining, making noises, taking things from others, getting up out of their seat), they can be encouraged to follow the rules of the class through explaining what you do want them to do and positive reinforcement, as opposed to 'telling them off' for doing inappropriate things.

Do check that behaviours are not part of the child's sensory regulation (e.g. humming or fiddling), and do assume that they may not understand the impact of what they are doing on their own or others' learning. It can be easy to assume they are doing it on purpose to be disruptive for the sake of being disruptive, trying to get out of doing something or trying to be in control. However, all behaviour has a 'purpose' and labelling a child as disruptive, sanctioning them or excluding them from the class or even school without supporting them does not help the child.

A useful strategy is a behaviour chart based on the child's interests, or more specifically a behaviour monitoring visual that explains exactly the positive

behaviours you want the child to try to show, which gives them a reward for doing the right thing. Being specific is much more successful than being general (e.g. 'be good' or 'be kind'). Begin with two to three 'rules', plus a self-esteem 'rule' to support the child's understanding that doing the right thing can be worth it.

A behaviour chart

Other ways of motivating appropriate behaviour can be through the child's visual timetable. Adding preferred activities (such as access to a sensory box or LEGO™ time) after a non-preferred activity can help a child get involved in a less favourite activity as they know that something better is coming after it. Consistency is key; when staff support these strategies consistently they can be very successful. An advantage of this way of motivating behaviour is that the child learns the valuable lesson that sometimes doing what they don't want to do has its rewards.

KS2

As a child's understanding of the behaviour expectations in school grow, it can still be difficult for them to keep *all* the rules *all* the time. That is too much for any child to achieve. The behaviours of a child with ASC are usually entirely logical to them, or in reaction to something they feel anxious, fearful, angry or excited about.

Sometimes teachers assume that KS2 children with ASC 'must know what to do by now' and so withdraw some of the communication, visual and sensory support that has been working so well. However, visual supports can still be very useful, although they do need to grow with the child. Children's interests change and their ability to understand classroom and work expectations and peer interactions may be different from what they understood in the earlier years. So as long as the support is there, we can have high expectations of what a child can achieve in terms of behaviour in school.

Case study

When Laura started Y5, staff felt that she didn't need her visual timetable any longer as she had hardly referred to it during the summer term of Y4. They also stopped doing her sensory breaks and began to give her more time to work without a teaching assistant (TA) nearby. The start of the year went well, but as the pace of work increased and the demands of the curriculum became more challenging, Laura's behaviour began to deteriorate. She started to display behaviours that the school hadn't seen since she was in Y2: refusing to do work, insisting all her pens and pencils were lined up on her desk, anxiety about getting everything right and arguments with her friends at playtime. All Laura said was *'I can't do it'* and refused to engage with her work each day.

With the help of a specialist teacher, the school looked at what her behaviours were communicating. Staff made a new, age-appropriate visual timetable for her, added sensory breaks twice a day and made sure that Laura had a clear way of communicating with the TA when she wanted help. Although these strategies had not been needed at the end of Y4, Laura needed them to help her overcome the extra demands and challenges of Y5 work.

Consequences and sanctions in KS2

A child with ASC who is able to see different points of view with support may also be taught about consequences and sanctions and how to cope with them. For example, by starting with the example of losing a game, children can be gently guided to understand that actions have different outcomes and that sometimes things that we do not want or like happen. It may take some time for a child to be able to cope with disappointment or other consequences, but teaching about it should always be reassuring and supportive. It is fine to teach that being rude to or hurting someone else wilfully is wrong and that children may receive a sanction for such behaviour. Sanctions need to be clear, short and meaningful to the child, and they work best when it has been agreed that it is a fair consequence with the child beforehand. They can help children understand that there can be negative consequences for wrong choices and positive consequences for good choices.

A social story can help explain what a consequence is. There is a difference between punishing the child and teaching them about sanctions; punishments tell the child they are 'wrong', whereas sanctions tell the child that there are usually consequences to their actions, for themselves and everyone else. To implement sanctions, you have to be consistent.

General classroom behaviour management for all Key Stages

There are many strategies you can use that are positive and directive responses to behaviour rather than negative reprimands or punishments. These reward the child with positive teacher attention.

> *Behaviour management interventions often come down to thinking ahead, being assertive and being confident.*
>
> Brown, 2015

Behaviour management also involves consistency and perseverance, so don't be too quick to think that something isn't working. Children with ASC may need a lot of practice to adjust their behaviour. Remember that ASC is a disability, and we have a responsibility to understand and meet the children's needs.

Top tips for supporting children with ASC

▶ ***Redirect inappropriate behaviour*** *by telling the child specifically what behaviour you do want.* 'Please sit quietly and listen to what I'm telling you.' *is better than* 'Behave yourself!' *or* 'Stop doing that.'

▶ ***Distract the child from inappropriate behaviour*** *by directing their focus onto their work and praising them for something they have achieved.*

▶ ***Give choices*** *rather than direct confrontation (e.g.* 'Do you want to sit quietly at your table or move to the workstation where you can work on your own?').

▶ ***Use special interests*** *to motivate the child. You may need to be quite creative but this can work very well.*

▶ ***Reduce sensory input*** *by allowing children to draw the blinds, wear headphones, or choose to sit where is most comfortable for them. Using fiddle toys may help some children feel calmer.*

▶ ***Adjust your language*** *by avoiding using the word* 'always' *(e.g.* 'We must always…') *as this sets impossible standards that no-one can keep. Use the words* 'sometimes' *and* 'usually' *instead. Use the word* 'finish' *instead of* 'stop'. *Make sentences shorter so you can pause more often, giving children processing time. Say what you mean clearly, without waffling or using sarcasm.*

▶ ***Come alongside*** *the child rather than confront them or stand over them, moving yourself to the side to speak to them.*

▶ ***Use a neutral tone of voice*** *and avoid shouting if you can. Even harsh or higher tones can cause much greater distress for a child with ASC.*

▶ ***Stay positive*** *by staying in control of your emotions and explain to the child what emotion you see them displaying (e.g.* 'It looks like you are frustrated with not being able to answer those maths questions. I'm here to help you. Tell me what you are struggling with.').

▶ ***Reduce pressure*** *on a child who is regularly not completing work, consider giving them less so that it can be achieved in the timeframe. Most teachers would rather have half a page completed by the child than two pages completed by the TA.*

▶ ***Don't assume*** *that children with ASC understand the impact their behaviour has on others. Explain it to them objectively, without accusation. Also let them explain the impact the behaviour of others has on them.*

▶ ***Keep changes to a minimum*** *by explaining and warning children with ASC when changes will happen where possible, and have a social story or written explanation of what to do if, for example, the teacher or room changes. Don't change your seating plan too often, and allow the children with ASC to stay in the same place or near the same people.*

▶ ***Label the behaviour not the child*** *by saying that you didn't like the behaviour or that it was the wrong thing to do, rather than imply in any way that the child themselves are wrong. Be aware of the child's sensitivity to their diagnosis. (This is also helpful for children who try to use their diagnosis as an excuse for their behaviour.)*

▶ ***Give children 'time out'*** *before things get too stressful. If you recognise that a child is feeling anxious then let them go out of class for a short while. They could go to a safe place, such as the learning support room or the library, or they could just be allowed to stand in the corridor for an agreed time. Alternatively, you could send the child on an errand to give them a break from the classroom. You may need a code between you and the child so they can ask for a break without it being obvious to others. Agree how long the break will last beforehand.*

▶ ***Use simple visuals*** *as these can make all the difference in helping a child remember what it is they are supposed to be doing. You can link visuals to their favourite characters or interests and make them amusing. This will help a child do the right thing and mean they are less likely to be shouted at because they can't remember what they should be doing when their brain is trying to process so many other things.*

Dealing with challenging behaviour

Although many children with ASC can follow rules and generally have no particular behaviour challenges, some frequently show challenging behaviours. It is important to understand that parents reporting challenging behaviour at home, even if this behaviour is not seen at school, is not necessarily a sign of poor parenting but is likely to be a sign that the child is not coping with school as well as it may seem.

It is also important to recognise that teachers and TAs often have an emotional and judgemental response to behaviours. We all have different tolerance levels and different views about what is acceptable or what is not. We can easily react to behaviours that make us feel angry or frustrated or that our authority is threatened. It is easy to end up in a power struggle with children if we feel that they are doing things deliberately to challenge us.

Generally, we feel that we can manage occasional behaviours and isolated incidents. However, behaviours that happen frequently, are repetitive, easily escalate or make every lesson with that child a battleground, can very quickly lead to serious and detrimental consequences for the child, with the focus being punishment rather than support. Common punishments often given to children with ASC include being sent to the headteacher, having to work outside the classroom, missing break times, and fixed-term or permanent exclusions. A whole-school strategy needs to be put in place early enough to prevent any of these things happening. The strategy should support the child so they can use appropriate communication and behaviour, however difficult a lesson, relationships or school in general is for them. Attempting to stop a behaviour without understanding the reason for it can only cause that behaviour to be replaced by another, often more disruptive behaviour (Moyes, 2013).

ASC behaviour is rarely about challenging the authority of the teacher, however much it may seem so initially. Most children with ASC have very logical reasons for their behaviour along with extreme stress and anxiety, and we need to discover what their reasons are by looking at their behaviour through an autistic perspective. If we take a step back without taking the behaviour personally and ask *'What is the child communicating through their behaviour?'*, then we are beginning to look at it in the most helpful way. The behaviour management approach then becomes pro-active and we can begin to look at what we can teach the child with ASC to help meet their needs in a more appropriate way.

Collecting evidence of behaviour

It can be difficult to get a wider view of a pupil's behaviour without speaking to other staff in the school. Some teachers believe that they have to sort it out themselves and that to ask for help is a sign of weakness. Actually, working together as a team is a professional strength and should be encouraged in all schools. The SENCO or senior leader may support you when a pupil's behaviour is impacting on their or others' learning.

First, information should be collected about the nature of the behaviour; how and when it is happening, what kind of responses are being used, and what effect they are having. Without having to fill in reams of paperwork, a simple form can be used to collect information about the function of the pupil's behaviour.

Remember that the child has a reason for their behaviour that is logical (to them). These reasons are usually linked to the child trying to meet a need that they have. Children can be very needs-driven and often find effective ways of getting their needs met. Children with ASC can find it difficult to adapt their behaviour without support as they may not have the thinking skills to work out what they can do instead. The main needs-driven behaviours can be grouped into four sections:

➤ **The need to get attention** (from adults or peers). This includes communicating they can't do something, wanting to join in but not knowing how, needing feedback or reassurance, and communicating that they are very anxious or fearful. A child with ASC may not have the communication or thought processing skills necessary to be able to tell you what is wrong.

➤ **The need to escape or avoid**. This includes others teasing them; noise, smells or other sensory overload; fear of a task or test; being overwhelmed by incidents, emotions or moods that may have nothing to do with your lesson; too many demands; feeling embarrassed, ill, hot or cold. They could also be bored, doing their least favourite subject, or may need a sudden change.

➤ **The need for sensory stimulation**. This includes fiddling, fidgeting, stroking, chewing, repetitive noises, singing, self-talk (i.e. talking to themselves during a solitary activity), tapping, flicking, rocking, climbing, spinning.

➤ **The need to get or have something**. This includes being unable to wait for something, unable to understand they will get a turn, anxiety about losing something, or fixations and obsessive interests.

Collecting information by talking to the child and observing them across a number of lessons and out-of-class situations can help us make a good guess as to what needs the behaviour is trying to meet. Parents should be consulted as to what they think may be the function of their child's behaviour and whether it is similar to their behaviour at home.

A STAR Record can be used by a teaching assistant (TA) shadowing the child (preferably without it being too obvious). It will note:

➤ the **S**etting (i.e. when and where these behaviours occur)

➤ the **T**riggers (i.e. what happens immediately before the behaviour)

➤ the **A**ctions of the pupil (i.e. what they actually did)

➤ the **R**esults of the behaviour (i.e. what happened immediately after the behaviour).

This is a helpful document and, along with the child's and their parents' comments, can help us gather enough information to support the next step: determining the information or skill that the child is missing in order to have their need met in an appropriate way.

This can be the key that unlocks the barriers the child has to appropriate behaviour, positive relationships and access to learning. The key to changing behaviour is to teach the child a skill which enables them to get their need met, to defer their need or to understand what else they could do in that situation. Sometimes it will be important for staff to support the child through it, and not seek to teach anything at that point; this is especially in the case of an emotional and sensory overload or meltdown.

Below are some case study examples of skills teaching that successfully changed a child's behaviour:

Hamed (Y2)

Behaviour	Hamed constantly interrupted his teacher and other adults, shouted out and demanded they look at what he had done.
Need	Hamed was seeking interaction. The problem was that all the feedback he was getting was negative.
Skill taught	A support programme was put in place to teach Hamed what waiting was and how to do it, with visual support. This was also practised by the parents who saw a great improvement in behaviour too.

Jonas (Y3)

Behaviour	Jonas pushed, kicked and nipped other pupils when lining up.
Need	Jonas wanted to escape out of the line and avoid going out of class. (This frequently worked.)
Skill taught	Jonas was anxious because he did not know where he was going. He was taught to ask 'Where are we going?' (Jonas, not the adult, was given the strategy to use.)

Suri (Y4)

Behaviour	Suri pushed, kicked and nipped other pupils when lining up.
Need	Suri wanted to escape out of the line and avoid going out of class. (This frequently worked.)
Skill taught	Suri was very sensitive to touch. She couldn't stand being in the line because others hurt her and it made her afraid. She was taught to wait to stand at the back of the line, and others were taught to allow her to do so.

Leanne (Y3)

Behaviour	Leanne always ran out of class to be first to pick up the football. She got very angry if she didn't get to it first, but then would not let anyone else have the ball.
Need	Leanne wanted to interact and play football but was too scared that no-one would pass the ball to her.
Skill taught	Leanne and her classmates were given lessons in how to play football together, by bringing in football coaches to school. A TA wrote the lessons into a social story for Leanne to take home, covering all the 'issues' she was worried about.

Gordon (Y2)

Behaviour	Gordon often ran out of class after throwing his work on the floor, screaming, crying and swearing at staff.
Need	Escape from the classroom was the way in which Gordon reacted to extreme emotional feelings that resulted from thinking the work was too hard for him. His screaming and swearing was his way of communicating that he was highly stressed.
Skill taught	Gordon was given some one-to-one mentoring sessions to help him understand emotions and visual support to communicate how he was feeling. A visual support to break down work tasks was used consistently in class and a programme of regular sensory breaks helped to manage his anxiety.

Behaviour support plans

Behaviour support plans enable all staff to work with parents to identify the key challenging behaviours and what proactive (preventative) strategies are going to be put in place at school, which can include suggested strategies for home too. It also sets out the reactive strategies to say what will be done when the challenging behaviours do happen. These may include low-level strategies such as redirecting, reminding of support and giving the child a break, as well as strategies for meltdowns if they are likely to occur. Any consequences for the child can be listed, as well as strategies for explaining these to the child. This document enables all staff (including welfare staff who are often left out of the picture despite spending an hour every day with the child) to be consistent, know who to ask for help and how to support the child positively. **See CD-ROM for a template of a behaviour support plan.**

Meltdowns, shutdowns and physical handling

A meltdown is a situation where the brain is so overwhelmed with stress chemicals, such as adrenalin and cortisone, that it goes into 'fight or flight' mode. This means that it has reached the point where it loses the ability to process new sensory and (most importantly) verbal information. The inability to process new verbal information is most important in this situation because the most common response to a child becoming so distressed is to talk to them and try to calm them down or redirect them. If they cannot comprehend what is being said, then the verbal noise will only serve to heighten their distress. If this happens to a child, their brain cannot respond to a situation (e.g. tell them to move, calm down). They will want to run or fight their way out of the classroom and verbal commands from a teacher, even in a soothing voice, can make things worse. They may physically attack equipment or others in the room as a result of feeling 'hemmed in' or threatened, showing the child feels unsafe and possibly terrified. The child will be trying to escape the source of stress, and teaching staff could be part of that stress if they try to approach the pupil to intervene. Children may also self-harm in an attempt to release the stress. This can may be a coping strategy to avoid hurting others or because they cannot escape from the situation.

Conversely, a child with ASC may not physically run or fight when they are in overload mode, but instead seem to shut down and be unresponsive. Some children may do this regularly unnoticed, and it's possible that staff think these moments are epileptic absences. It may be that parents will want to refer their child to their GP to check if epilepsy may be present or to rule it out.

To help a child who is in meltdown or shutdown mode, there are three key principles to remember:

1 Silence

Don't bombard the child with verbal language. Often we panic too and our voices can seem harsh or be loaded with emotion and panic. Only use the minimum verbal language necessary in a calm and reassuring tone to direct other children away from the situation, other staff to stand back and the child with ASC to a safe place. Once the child is in a safe place, be silent so they do not have to process verbal language. Visuals can be used to communicate that they are okay, are being helped and can take the time they need to recover. A child's aggression often subsides when you back off, remove demands (especially social and interaction demands) and give them space. If you stand too near, you may be putting yourself in danger.

2 Safety

The safety of the child and others must be paramount. If a child has had one or more meltdowns or shutdowns, then work out where a safe place is beforehand. Allocate a place and plan for the event of a meltdown or shutdown, inform all staff of the plan and follow it calmly.

3 Recovery

The child who has had a meltdown or shutdown will need time for their brain to recover. This may involve them going home or staying in the safe place for some time until they feel able to re-join the class. They may like to be wrapped in a blanket, hide under a cushion or sit in the dark. Some may fall asleep because of the exhaustion a meltdown or shutdown causes. This is not a situation in which you should try to go over the incident with the child, exclude them or punish them.

The best way to deal with meltdowns or shutdowns is to be aware of what may trigger them, and then avoid them. Have a plan in place and share it with the child and their parents to help the child know that if they become distressed they will be helped and supported rather than punished and blamed.

By law, teachers are allowed to use 'reasonable force' in certain circumstances for the sake of the child and their own safety. Teachers need to be aware of the law and schools should have a policy that explains this and supports children and staff in staying safe.

The most recent document *Statement on restrictive physical interventions with children* from The Challenging Behaviour Foundation (2016) states:

> *NHS England (2015) is clear that 'support and interventions should always be provided in the least restrictive manner. Where an individual needs to be restrained in any way – either for their own protection or the protection of others, restrictive interventions should be for the shortest possible and using the least restrictive means possible.*

If a member of staff has ever found themselves needing to physically remove a child with ASC from a situation, they should go to their Senior Leadership Team and insist on a Positive Behaviour Support Plan which will form part of the child's IEP and will identify exactly how this situation will be handled in any future cases, and put in place as many preventative strategies as possible. Parents must be included and ideally all staff should receive behaviour training. This may include some training on safe handling. Teachers and TAs should never be left in a position where they are having to frequently carry a child out of class or hold them to prevent them hurting themselves or others.

CHAPTER 10
Social interaction and developing friendships

Primary school is a huge social minefield for children with Autism Spectrum Condition (ASC). The demands to interact with others from the moment they approach the school gates and throughout almost every moment of the day are constant and there are many overwhelming social challenges to contend with which require social skills that the child may not have developed yet.

> *Non-autistic children usually learn all these social skills in an unconscious and intuitive way, by observing and interacting with everyone around them. The tendency of children on the autism spectrum to focus on 'detail' instead of the overall 'plot' means they are usually better off learning these social skills in a more concrete way.*
>
> **www.autism-help.org**

Children with ASC have a social impairment at the core of their diagnosis. Their brains struggle to process social information. Observing what is happening, extracting the important information from what they see, interpreting it and knowing what the appropriate response is can be overwhelming for a child with ASC. Neurotypical children will do this unconsciously most of the time and can react almost instantly to a situation. Of course, all children start school with immature skills which will grow and develop through their primary years, but children with ASC have a greater naivety and lack of awareness or understanding. They can have difficulties with:

➤ **Social interaction**
This includes understanding what is happening in context, knowing how to respond, using the right communication skills and taking other people's feelings and viewpoints into account. Not knowing how to interact socially can make it very hard to form friendships.

➤ **Social communication**
This includes understanding what is being communicated not only in words but also in gestures, facial expressions, tone of voice and context. It involves recognising when someone is approaching you, wanting to interact with you and what their intentions might be. It also involves recognising when someone is being sarcastic, joking or teasing you. Children with ASC can be hindered by their literal understanding and lack of ability to read non-verbal communication. Social communication also encompasses knowing the words needed to talk to others, understanding the two-way nature of conversation, being able to join in, knowing

what topics people might like to talk about and following the flow of a one-to-one or group conversation.

➤ **Social imagination**
This includes the ability to understand and predict other people's intentions and behaviour, and to imagine situations outside of one's own regular experiences.
This may be difficult for a child who has a narrow, repetitive range of activities and obsessions and tends to dominate a conversation or activity.

Attwood (2006) considers that there are three types of social characters in those with ASC. These are noted below:

Introverted, isolated and withdrawn

In primary schools, these children will be those who would rather do anything than sit or work with others. They feel much safer staying away from other people and can be very vulnerable to being ignored, left out and even bullied. They are often highly anxious.

Intrusive, intense and abrasive

These children won't read the signals for when to consider others or change what they are doing, and are often in conflict with others through arguments or fighting. They want to be in the middle of a crowd, the centre of attention and in control of what the group does. They do not like it when others make suggestions and can become angry, abusive or violent if things don't go their way. Most of their interactions and relationships are superficial or based on intense common interests. They may be loud and brash and take lots of risks with words and actions because they lack the social skills needed to have proper conversations and more mature interactions.

Observant, analytical and imitating

Many of these children will be girls. They won't understand social situations intuitively but will have developed an enormous capacity to copy what others are doing. In the Early Years and KS1, this may have been enough for these children to get by, but as social relationships and interests become increasingly complex in the KS2 years, they will start to seem awkward and out of place (even in their friendship groups). This may be why many girls with autism are not diagnosed until much later than boys. As school progresses, they may be increasingly left out and not know why, or become the target of teasing. Their imitating behaviour may become obsessive to the point of copying another person's mannerisms, clothing and interests.

Many skills are needed in order to be able to interact successfully with others and these become increasingly complex as children get older. The skills to negotiate a variety of relationships are vital to be able to function in adult life. Primary schools need to start to provide support to build up social interaction skills and confidence in children with ASC in order to fully meet their needs. This will form part of any Education, Health and Care (EHC) Plan the child may have. This support needs to be structured and personalised for each child throughout their time at primary school.

It is important to respect the child's individuality and remember that we are not forcing them to 'be like everyone else', or giving them a set of rigid 'rules' for how to behave around others.

Children with ASC need skills and coping strategies to enable them to deal with other people in different situations, have successful friendships and relationships and know how to keep themselves safe from being exploited and bullied, whilst knowing that being who they are and having ASC are entirely acceptable. It is important to respect their desires not to get involved in social activities or that it is okay to withdraw themselves from a situation they are uncomfortable with, and teach them that this is acceptable too.

It is a myth that children with ASC don't want friends. It may be that some are happy in their own company and find other people too confusing and stressful to be with. They should be taught that preferring their own company is acceptable. However, some children with ASC do want to have friendships, but often find themselves without friends. Not only do their social communication impairments cause difficulties, but often other children are a barrier to them developing friendships too. Other pupils' reactions to the interests, behaviours and differences of children with ASC can be negative, teasing and dismissive. The fear, anger and sadness that results from this can cause a child with ASC to become more aggressive or withdrawn and so the isolation and loneliness increases. This experience is far too common for children with ASC.

The social naivety of children with ASC can make them vulnerable to being made fun of, taken advantage of and bullied by others who they think are their friends. Children with ASC may look towards adults for friendship, but their peers are better role models for social situations and understanding, and can bring the benefits of true friendship. A peer friendship can help a child with ASC learn how to act in different situations and how to deal with conflict or unsafe situations, usually when no adult is present. A peer who shares the same interests and sense of humour with a child with ASC can make a great difference to break times and lunchtimes. A child with ASC can be a good and loyal friend and offer just as much to a friendship. As with all people, a good friend provides comfort and hope when things go wrong, and affirms you and encourages you. Usually, schools look for peers for children with ASC in their own year group, but it may be worth giving them the opportunity to find peers of all ages through special interest groups and clubs within the school.

Early Years

Social skills in the Early Years are best taught through teaching play skills. Shared attention can be taught through using the child's favourite and familiar toys and games as an adult and other children play alongside them, imitating the play with a similar toy (e.g. if a child who is lining up cars can see that someone else is lining up their cars in a similar way, they will hopefully be interested in what they are doing).

Many skills, like taking turns, can be explained in small achievable steps. It may often be the case that situations in which we can teach skills such as turn-taking, waiting and listening have to be engineered. A social skills programme should be a discrete but integral part of the support that is given to the child. Wherever possible, it should be part of a child's everyday activities, but it can also be taught through fun structured games and activities. A programme to support social skills in the Early Years can include:

➤ **Activities with another child and a supporting adult.** These can include parallel play, singing rhymes and doing actions in front of a full-length mirror (this is good for self-awareness). Rhymes that need two (e.g. *See-saw* and *Row, row, row your boat* rhymes) can be good to introduce shared actions and are fun. Outdoor play activities such as taking turns pulling each other on a pull-along vehicle, pushing each other on a swing and carrying something together can also encourage positive peer interactions for all children.

➤ To develop imaginative play, teach **roleplay and dressing up**. The adult may have to model and demonstrate at first (e.g. show how to carry a bag of letters or parcels as a postman). Props such as a train driver's hat, masks of favourite TV characters or a fireman's hose may go down well. Linking these props to the interests of the child with ASC works well. It is good to have a full-length mirror available so the child can watch themselves 'pretending'

➤ **Puppets** can be appealing to some children with ASC, especially if they are related to their interests. Sometimes children like to operate the puppet themselves, and it can become a way in which they interact with their peers. Puppets can also model social scenarios for the child to learn from, such as how to say hello to someone or how to ask to join in a play activity

➤ **A structured programme** (such as *Time to Talk* by Alison Schroeder) is a good way of introducing social skills group activities in the Early Years and KS1

In the Early Years classroom, friendships are developed through all children learning how to get along with each other, whatever their abilities and needs. A child with ASC may miss out on budding friendships if their behaviour is unpredictable or alarming to other children. If this is the case, the priority should be to support them to feel less anxious and be able to navigate the activities and demands of the classroom more confidently.

> *Many children with ASC go through the whole of primary school with a loyal and helpful peer group who accept them and understand their needs, along with a few close friends who have similar interests and can cope with each other's differences.*

> *However, unless the issue of acceptance and understanding is addressed in these formative years, children with ASC can become increasingly left out, not invited to parties and avoided by their peers.*

KS1 & KS2

Teachers will assume that children in KS1 will have acquired a certain level of social development, and this is even more acute in KS2 when academic development becomes much more important. Social skills are extremely complex and it takes a long time for children to learn the skills they need to interact with others successfully, even when they do not have ASC. Indeed, we continue to learn social interaction skills into adulthood. Attwood (2006) identifies the essential skills for making friends as:

➤ Being able to join other children's activities.

➤ Allowing and tolerating other children joining your own games or activities.

➤ Recognising when you need help and seeking help from others.

➤ Understanding when and how to help others, and seeing that as valuable to the friendship.

➤ Giving compliments at the right times and knowing how to respond to compliments.

➤ Knowing the right time to criticise and appropriate ways of phrasing negative comments, and knowing when to hold back from criticising.

    ➤ Being able to accept criticism from others and adapt behaviour accordingly.

    ➤ Incorporating the ideas and suggestions of others into an activity.

    ➤ Keeping on topic, allowing others to have their say in conversation.

    ➤ Managing disagreement with negotiation and compromise.

    ➤ Understanding that it is acceptable for others to have different opinions to yours.

    ➤ Understanding and 'reading' facial expressions and body language.

    ➤ Showing empathy with others in both positive and negative situations.

    ➤ Being able to get out of a situation and end a conversation appropriately.

An observation and checklist of the child with ASC's abilities and areas of difficulty should be made so that a programme can be built based on the child's needs. What they can do can be celebrated, developed and generalised, and new skills can be learned through direct teaching and practice across contexts to support generalisation. Many commercial social skills programmes begin with a child questionnaire. Alternatively, **see CD-ROM for a social communication checklist** for KS1–2 to be used at the initial assessment stage.

A social skills programme from KS1–KS2

Children with ASC benefit from a structured social skills programme throughout their years at school. A structured social skills programme should be flexible, taught, roleplayed and practised, and give the children ownership of their own learning and development and a chance to evaluate it.

Implementing a social skills programme needs flexibility from the school. Time will need to be set aside for these sessions, and a mixture of group work and individual work may be needed. Sessions will need to be regular and provide opportunities for generalising taught skills in regular classes and unstructured times. Often, a teaching assistant (TA) or nurture teacher may lead these sessions, or a school may buy in a specialist teacher to do so. Schools may run these sessions in assembly time, break times, lunchtimes or during lesson time, depending on the needs of the children.

There are many good resources available to purchase which provide structured teaching plans, resources and group activity ideas that are practical and relevant. It is a good idea to choose at least two programmes and personalise them to the child/children. This gives more ideas to work with and a greater bank of resources to draw from over the child's primary school years. It is important to be flexible, so that issues raised by the children can be explored in the following session rather than left for a long time. When choosing a programme, look for photocopiable resources, clear and chunked information and visuals to support the learning concepts. *Time to Talk* and *Socially Speaking*, both by Alison Schroeder, are both great programmes with excellent board games that support the skills the children are learning. Alternatively, you could make your own.

Children with ASC should be taught about skills, and then given the opportunity to look for examples of situations in which they can be used and when they or others already use these skills. Give them many opportunities to practise these skills in different contexts, including at home. It is important to develop self-awareness and self-esteem during these programmes, and for children to understand their ASC, and know that it doesn't mean that anything is wrong with them. The more the child contributes to the sessions with their own ideas, the more they will learn from them.

Building on the basics

Children with ASC have an uneven development in their social understanding and skills. They may not yet have developed some important foundational social skills; indeed, the nature of ASC means that some individuals will not develop all of the skills they need through into adulthood. Making eye contact may be difficult for them throughout their life. Understanding small talk or casual chatting may never make sense to them, and approaching others may always be the most uncomfortable and stressful thing they do in their lives. It is important to keep this in mind when delivering a social skills programme. Allow children to learn at their own pace and give them the means with which to express their own views. Providing structure and explanations of what the key social skills are can be a good way to encourage their self-awareness and learning.

Begin with finding out what the child can do, what they are beginning to learn and what skills they are unable to do, then design sessions based on what they may need to learn and allow the children to contribute to the plans. Board and card games are a good way for many children with ASC to begin to learn social skills. They are not perceived as work and, if taught and structured well, they can provide lots of opportunity to practise the skills being taught. These five skills are a good place to start; greeting, looking, listening, waiting and what to say.

The teacher can give points to the children when they notice them using the skills and children should be encouraged to notice the skills in themselves and each other. For example, the teacher may pause and ask *'Has anyone seen someone doing good listening? You can give them a point.'* The points are added in the form of a tally chart on the skills board and earned towards whatever reward the group decides on (either individual or shared). Children might enjoy working towards extra playtimes, stickers, certificates or prizes. As long as the reward is motivating to them, you can use your imagination.

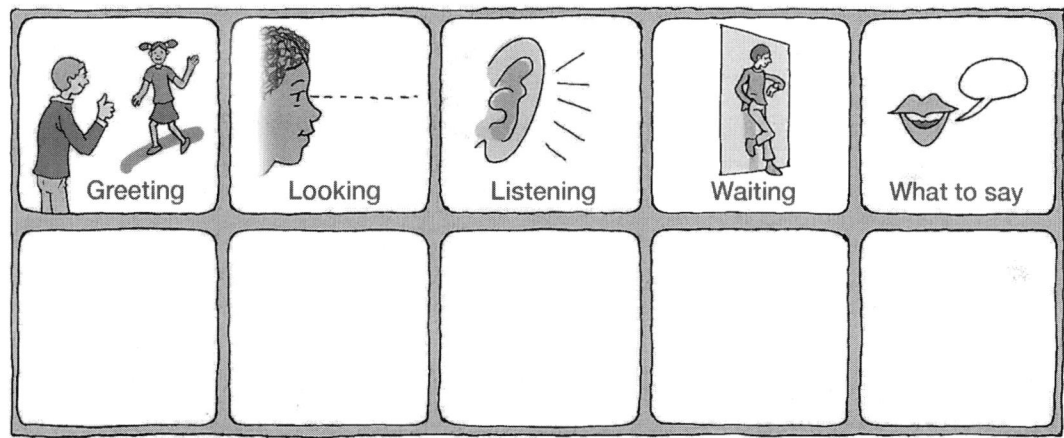

Social skills board. See CD-ROM for printable resource.

Playing a variety of social skills and encouraging the children to practise these skills in their lessons will encourage generalisation of the skills. So if the focus is listening skills, staff and children will be looking for examples of good listening throughout the week. The five basic skills above can be a focus of a whole term's group work and be shared with parents as homework.

Moving on: conversation skills

Conversations happen all around us. Children with ASC may have difficulty starting a conversation, joining in or knowing how to end it. They may not be able to tell when someone is bored, teasing or being sarcastic. They may interrupt or want to talk about their interests and opinions all the time. Showing how a conversation can be structured, the kinds of topics that different people discuss and how to start, continue and end a conversation can be useful skills for all children.

Children with ASC don't always understand that a conversation is a sharing of ideas and opinions and that it is possible to disagree with someone without arguing or destroying a friendship. It is a good idea to begin with a definition of what a conversation is and how it works in a structured session. The children can do this themselves.

Children may need to do some work on:

> ➤ How to start and end a conversation
> ➤ Asking and answering questions, waiting for a response and what to respond with
> ➤ Exploring different kinds of questions (open-ended; closed; *what, where, why, when, how* and *who* questions) and which are more effective

Topic cards can be used to help children choose what to start talking about. The more the children with ASC make suggestions and give their own ideas, the more they will be able to develop their own understanding of social communication. It is important to teach how to leave a conversation politely for situations where children feel under pressure, overloaded or uncomfortable. In order to be successful, work on conversations may need to take place over the course of a whole school year and be refreshed in subsequent school years. Work with children on this topic regularly, starting in KS2 once the earlier skills have been well embedded.

Learning to read non-verbal communication

Children with ASC who have the most awareness that they cannot understand others and who are interested in interacting with others often get frustrated. They don't automatically understand what to do in many social situations, or indeed, why other people do what they do. However, they are able to learn about more complex communication and social skills that can help them navigate the complexities of relationships at school as well as in their families and community. If a child with ASC is able and ready, they can learn about how to 'read' other people and social situations through becoming a 'social detective' (or for a science-focused child, a 'social scientist').

Being a social detective

It is important to teach children with ASC that there are no definite 'right' or 'wrong' answers. Social reading is like being a detective or scientist. The reader looks for evidence and clues, then makes a good guess as to what the other person thinks, intends or means based on the evidence and clues. Many children will treat this as a game or challenge. This may always be a difficult concept for children with ASC to grasp, but they can learn to understand social situations better with practice. Whereas neurotypical children have a natural capacity to make good guesses about what is happening in a social sense (although they sometimes get it wrong too!), children with ASC will have to work hard at this. Good friends and peers can be invaluable in helping them with this. It may be useful to have some neurotypical peers in the group, as long as they do not dominate the discussions.

Aspects of social communication children with ASC could learn about through being a social detective include:

> ➤ 'reading' people (i.e. their facial expressions, body language and posture) (*What are people telling us non-verbally? How can we guess what their intentions might be?*)
> ➤ emotions (*How do people display these? What are appropriate responses?*)
> ➤ sarcasm, humour and jokes
> ➤ inference, slang and idioms

➤ context (an important social reading skill) (*What is happening around the incident? What are the context clues?*)

➤ intonation, pitch and volume of speech and how these are interpreted

➤ different types of questions, and which are most useful and when

➤ manners, assertiveness, arguments and communication breakdowns (*How do we know people are bored or want to leave the conversation?*)

➤ online safety and appropriate things to share online (taking time to understand clues before replying) (*How much is too much? When should we ignore?*). For symbol-based SMART internet rules see www.childnet.com/resources/know-it-all-for-teachers-sen/symbols-based-smart-rules

➤ trust, keeping safe and how to get out of uncomfortable or threatening situations (including online)

➤ character (*How do we assess someone's character from the way they behave?*)

There is enough in this list to keep going long after a child has left primary school! You can use many techniques to teach these skills and for most children with ASC they should include:

➤ visual pictures of real-life situations

➤ social stories

➤ video clips

➤ roleplay

➤ games

➤ problem-solving activities

➤ projects to work on alone, with a partner or in a group

➤ mapping ideas out to see connections between them

➤ puppets

LEGO™ Therapy

A recent initiative has been the use of LEGO to teach and practise social skills. LEGO has the advantage of being highly motivating to many children and is seen as a play rather than a work activity. LEGO Therapy (2014) teaches social skills through providing structure and allocating roles to the children in a group so that they must communicate with each other and work together to complete a task. Challenge cards (either made by the children or teaching staff, or available already made on the internet which encourage children to work either individually or together to build a particular model (such as a robot, house or vehicle). The Lego Therapy model is to then introduce the following job descriptions which can be chosen be the children or allocated by the teacher:

➤ The **architect** or **designer** decides what the group is going to build. (You can support this with choice cards).

➤ The **supplier** receives instructions from the designer and gets the bricks needed from the box, then passes them to the builder.

➤ The **builder** receives instructions from the designer and builds the model.

➤ Other roles can be introduced, such as **supervisor**, who is in charge of making sure everyone is working together.

LEGO Therapy is a great way to develop social skills such as:

- communicating instructions
- waiting
- patience with others
- sharing attention
- listening
- learning to negotiate.

It also develops a shared enjoyment and pride in a job completed. Arguments between children can be used as an opportunity to discuss how to deal with different opinions and how to compromise.

Teaching about emotions

Many children with ASC find it difficult to understand emotions and communicate to others what they are feeling. It is a myth to say that children with ASC do not have empathy or feelings. The difficulty is that feelings are likely to be intense, sudden and/or totally confusing.

However, children with ASC may pay much less attention to other people's faces and their emotional expressions because of poor eye contact and other skills (such as shared attention) not developing in a typical way. They may not be able to recognise that someone is happy, sad or angry through their tone of voice, behaviour and body language and may respond inappropriately (such as laughing when someone has hurt themselves) or not at all.

Others may find expressions of emotion so overwhelming that they withdraw, hit out or become scared because they don't know how to react. This confusion, paired with social communication difficulties, can mean that they do not show concern for others, comfort them or share in social emotion (such as sadness at someone dying). They can also be prone to misinterpreting emotional signs and often respond in odd or unexpected ways.

Children with ASC may have face-blindness or scan faces in a different way to neurotypical children. For example, they may focus on the mouth or another part of the face rather than the eyes, which are often the key to reading an emotion and can tell us more about the actions of the rest of the face (e.g. the action of moving the mouth could be a smile of pleasure or a grimace).

Children with ASC will need to be taught about emotions through modelling, demonstrating and explaining. Label emotions in natural contexts as they interact, play, read stories and do activities. You can comment on the child's own emotional state and that of others (e.g. *'Look, George is happy, he's smiling.'*, *'I'm feeling okay today. I'm calm and relaxed.'*, *'You look angry, can I help you?'*).

Emotional literacy

Giving the child some emotional vocabulary can help them express their emotional state. The first emotion words might include *happy, sad, angry, okay, excited, worried* and *calm*.

Attwood (2014) states that children with ASC often are so anxious all the time that 'okay' and 'calm' are emotions they are rarely aware of. Sensory and non-demanding activities can be ideal situations to teach them what okay and calm feel like.

> *Having the word* calm *in their vocabulary and understanding that it is a desirable state for them can help a child seek out self-calming activities. So many children are told to 'calm down' without staff knowing whether they understand what that means.*

The next stage of learning emotional literacy is becoming familiar with some of the other words we use to describe emotions and how we define them. There are many words we use for emotions and these can be grouped together to describe an emotion's intensity. For example, *annoyed, angry,* and *in a rage* show different intensities of anger. Some good resources for this can be found at www.do2learn. com. This vocabulary can help an older child communicate their feelings adequately, and help them know that we often feel more than one emotion at a time (e.g. we can be shocked and happy or angry and frustrated simultaneously). Use visuals and charts to support emotional literacy, but be aware of teaching emotions in context to develop childrens' social understanding of emotions.

Friendship support

A child with ASC who is really struggling to make and sustain friendships can be supported by a buddy system, particularly at playtimes, or by a very structured programme called *Circle of Friends*.

Buddy system

A buddy system can be much less formal than *Circle of Friends* and consists of the child with ASC choosing and asking between three and six other children to be in their 'buddy group'. Each playtime or class activity time, the child can choose a buddy from their group to work or play with. A visual choice board should support this, and clear rules explained as to how it will work. Rules should include that it's okay if someone doesn't want to play today (although consent should be gained from the other children in the buddy group that they will say yes to a request to buddy whenever possible). Having a few other children in their buddy group can help a child with ASC develop the ability to share friends and interact with a wider circle of children than they might otherwise. Remember, buddies can also include children from other classes at playtimes.

Circle of Friends

Circle of Friends is an approach in which a teacher-led group of children are selected to be trained and supported to become befrienders of a child with ASC. The group needs to be monitored and the children should meet regularly to discuss issues, problem-solve and be trained as supporters. *Circle of Friends* requires the permission of the parents of all children who are to be involved.

Whittaker et al. (1998) outline the four main aims of *Circle of Friends* as:

1 Creating a support network for the focus child.
2 Providing the child with encouragement and recognition for any achievements and progress.
3 Working with the child to identify difficulties and devising practical ideas to help deal with these difficulties.
4 Helping to put these ideas into practice.

For more details about setting up this programme go to the autism website – www.autism.org.uk

Making the best of playtimes

There are many challenges for a child with ASC in the playground. These can include:

➤ The child wants to be on their own, and needs 'down time'

➤ Misunderstanding competitive elements of games (winning and losing can be a problem)

➤ Literal understanding of language causing confusion

➤ Lots of people all talking at once, often whilst moving around, leading to difficulty 'tuning in'

➤ The child does not know how to ask to play

➤ Other children may not approach the child with ASC, or give up if they don't respond

➤ The child has tried to join in and failed many times, so they give up

➤ Friendship groups may change

➤ It can be difficult for a child with ASC to know who is approachable and what they are doing

➤ The child may not understand the concept of personal belongings, and may take things off others (leading to conflict)

➤ The child may not understand imaginative games, find it difficult to contribute ideas, or want only their own ideas to be implemented

➤ There can be too many social situations to read all at once, resulting in difficulty focusing

➤ There can be a wide range of ages and unfamiliar children in the playground

➤ Not knowing the wider social rules of the playground (e.g. the younger children do not go near the Y6 football match!)

➤ The playground is a much bigger area than they are used to with children constantly moving around (affecting visual-spatial perception)

➤ There is too much that is unpredictable so the child with ASC may retreat into obsessive or ritualistic behaviours to cope

➤ The child may want to follow rigid rules and have no flexibility when others want to change or vary things

➤ Anxiety levels can be very high, leading to panic and/or aggression

➤ Timing of playtimes may change and the child may not be able to cope with this

➤ The child may be too dependent on an adult helper and so less likely to approach peers independently

➤ They may have sensory overload in the playground

Teachers and teaching assistants (TAs) need to have breaks, but a child with ASC may need extra support at playtimes, meaning that an adult may need to be available out on the playground as part of the support offered. This should be not only so they can intervene when things go wrong but also implement and teach supportive strategies for successful play and interaction.

Playtime strategies

➤ In low-level incidents where children have bumped into each other or there is no obvious hurt, try to distract all children involved and redirect them to continue to play. (Some children may enjoy another getting into trouble for even minor incidents.)

➤ If a child is hurt by someone (e.g. by specific hitting, pushing, kicking):

  ▸ Ask the child to stand by you and send all children not involved in the incident away.
  ▸ Tell the child that hitting is not a good way to play and that we need to sort it out by saying sorry.
  ▸ Allow the child time to say sorry to the other and then tell them both that it has now been sorted.
  ▸ Ask the children how they can get back to playing a good game and send them back to play.

▸ If any children cannot continue playing without conflict, give both pupils 'time out' for two minutes by the wall. Don't talk to them during this time. Once two minutes have passed, tell them the issue has been sorted and that they can go and play again.

▸ It is not a good idea to try to talk too much or investigate each situation fully. Situations will resolve quickest if you are calm, follow the above script and do not use too many words.

▸ Any more serious incidents than these should be reported to the class teacher at the end of playtime.

A child who needs to spend time alone at playtimes can be allowed to do so, but should also be gradually introduced to shared activities based on things they like and find fun, and that they are successful in. A class or school topic about playground games can be a good way to support the whole class or school about the variety of games they can play. A good way to transfer this into the playground is to make 'game bags'. These are a bit like a story bag and include a copy of the game rules (in photos, pictures or written form) and the equipment needed.

Outdoor and environmental play activities, such as Forest Schools, can be a great way for children with ASC to develop friendships, social skills and positive shared experiences, and can tap into their special interests.

Case study

Musa (Y3 pupil) was encouraged to use his interest in Mario Kart™ games to invent an obstacle course using the playground play equipment, which many children really enjoyed along with him.

When accessing training about ASC and developing playground play activities, remember to include welfare staff. This can be a valuable investment for schools as well-trained welfare staff can help lunchtimes (when children are outside for long periods of time each day) run smoothly.

Wet playtimes

For children with ASC, wet playtimes can either be a delight (because they hate going outside) or a trauma (because it is a change to the normal routine). The key is to be prepared for them and have a structured plan in place which is communicated to all staff as well as the child with ASC.

Recommendations:

▸ Prepare and have resources ready (e.g. interests box, choice board).
▸ Teach structure and clear expectations through social stories.
▸ Have a 'time out' option planned and made clear to the child.
▸ Consider giving the child jobs to do or a quiet place to go.

CHAPTER 11
Supporting change and transition

I feel afraid. Like, 'What will happen now? What will I do now? What will other people do now? Will I understand what is going to happen instead of what was supposed to happen? Will I be able to do what I need to do now, as I would have been able to if things hadn't changed?'

Johnston & Hatton, 2016

We know that life is full of small and big changes, that nothing stays the same for long and that we cannot stop the world around us from changing. Dealing with change involves us having to first imagine and try to **predict** what it might involve (based on our previous knowledge and experience) and then make a **plan** as to how we are going to deal with it. We then need to be able to **organise** and carry out the plan, and **allow for adaptations** as we go along. Most of the time, we have an emotional response to change, including expectation, excitement, anxiety and panic. Changes (especially unexpected changes) can be welcomed or stressful.

Children with Autism Spectrum Condition (ASC) have difficulty with **flexible thinking** which affects their ability to imagine what something will be like, make organised plans and to monitor those plans to effect a successful outcome. They may also have difficulty understanding the **concept of time**, so worrying about when something will happen and how long it will take (and will life *ever* get back to normal?) will also add to their anxiety. All of these skills (and others) are needed to cope with change effectively.

This is why sometimes seemingly small and common changes can be overwhelming for children with ASC. Things such as being asked to try new activities or foods they have never eaten before, or changing clothes for PE, can lead to refusal, distress or tantrums. Even a teacher changing their appearance (even in a relatively minor way such as by tying their hair back) can throw a child with ASC completely.

Some children with ASC insist on certain things being done in the same order all the time and cannot cope if, for instance, someone is absent and doesn't reply to their name on the register. The change to the absolute sameness that they crave can affect a child's ability to sleep as their brain cannot make the transition from 'on' to 'off', and changes like buying new clothes, taking a different route home or buying a different brand of food can create havoc for parents.

The need for routine, sameness and rituals can be very strong in some children with ASC. It can pose quite a challenge in the classroom as the need to move, adapt, share and change, as well as the unpredictability of other people, can cause challenging behaviours as the child tries desperately to control their environment.

A child's lack of flexibility in their imagination can mean that they don't 'get' commonplace things (for example, that a red pencil can be used for the same purpose as the blue pencil they usually use – and are distressed about because it is missing), and teachers often don't understand the problem (in this example, why the child won't use the red pencil instead). Transition from an activity a child with ASC is enjoying to a non-preferred or new activity can cause refusal and distress, as can having longer assemblies, visitors in school, doing things in a different order to usual or having a substitute teacher in class can all be challenging for these children, and can turn into a battleground between a teacher or TA and a child.

The key is to try to understand the situation from the child's point of view and to plan for changes and help prepare them to cope with changes. Obviously, it is impossible to plan for all changes as there are many times they are unexpected, sudden and out of our control, but a child can be taught that even unexpected changes can be coped with.

Small changes and bigger changes, such as a new class, a new baby in the family, going for a doctor's appointment, a special assembly or a residential trip, can be prepared for using a number of familiar strategies:

➤ Teach new ways of doing the same thing, or using familiar toys and objects in new ways through demonstration. It may take a while before the child will have a go at this themselves but it can be a valuable skill for them to learn, particularly if they have poor imagination or transference skills. Visual support can help

➤ Put any changes on the child's visual timetable in advance, if possible. If the change is a longer time away, use a calendar so each day leading up to it can be ticked off. (Only do this if the child can cope with a long wait for the event to happen. Some children may cope better if they don't have too much time to worry about it.)

➤ Place a *surprise* or ? symbol on the timetable and make sure that at first the ? activity is something the child enjoys so that they learn to associate the symbol with a pleasant experience. Do this daily at first

➤ Acknowledge the child's worries and anxiety and that it is acceptable to feel that way. Praise them and tell them that they have been 'flexible' when they do cope with something unexpected. Introduce them to being 'proud' of themselves when they try something new

➤ Give warning of unexpected and sudden events such as a fire drill wherever possible.

➤ Prepare them for a new experience as well as possible. You could use a booklet or social story about what it will be like, ask visitors (e.g. a visiting author) to email photos of themselves or look at a website or video of a place you will be visiting – or even better, do some pre-visit visits

➤ Give more time for the child with ASC to process moving from one activity to another. Use a timer to help them prepare for the move and know when it will be happening

➤ Give the child sensory and/or favoured objects for them to take with them from one activity to another. If holding onto something will affect them doing the activity, provide a special place for the object to rest in the child's view whilst they do the activity

➤ If possible, involve the child in planning changes and give them some choices and control over what happens, such as where they will sit, what they can take with them and how long they will have to stay there

➤ Have a one-page profile of the child (a Child Passport) prepared for the event of a supply teacher covering your class. Include the main ways to engage with the child, what helps them and what not to do. **See CD-ROM for a child passport template.**

➤ Work with parents to support major changes at home (e.g. family break-up, moving house, going to the dentist) using these strategies

Case study

Amena (Y6 pupil) went on a residential trip. She made a booklet about it beforehand using the previous year's photos, and staff made her a visual keyring for each day with the routine and activities on so she could keep it in her pocket to refer to whenever she was anxious. This included the *?* symbol for free time.

Be aware that certain times of the year are full of change at school and in the community. Christmas in particular is full of changes, which can lead to lots of unsettlement, anxiety and even challenging behaviour from a child with ASC. These seasonal changes include lights appearing everywhere, the excitement and anxiety about receiving unknown gifts (which can be a major worry for some children; do not assume they like Christmas) and the normal school routine being apt to change suddenly every day as play practices and arts and crafts activities replace the usual work. During this time, keep the routine as clear as possible. Put things like play practices on a child's visual timetable and support them as much as possible with calming and routine activities.

SATs week and the end of the school year can pose similar challenges. The key is to understand this and be prepared.

Transition to the next class in September

Moving class signifies a change and a move into the unknown for a child with ASC. Some children may cope well with the same transition experience that the rest of the class have, but many will need extra support and planning to be able to make the transition successfully. The best strategies include involving the child in meeting and getting to know their new teacher, allowing them to become familiar with the classroom, and giving them choices such as choosing where they will sit and which coat peg will be theirs.

Making a transition book full of photos and information that children with ASC can take home to read during the summer holiday can be really helpful. A schedule of the first day back at school after the holiday can be added to this or sent to the child's home before the start of the new academic year.

The child will need to know what will be the same, as well as what will be new. The more that will be familiar to them, the better they will feel. Now is not the time to make major changes without the child's consent. Therefore, if they have always used a particular cushion to sit on, or had a photo visual timetable, keep this the same across the transition. If you want to make any changes (e.g. change the photo visual timetable to symbols), either make them whilst the child is still in their 'old' class or wait until they have settled into their new one.

Transition to secondary school

A successful transition from primary to secondary school starts as early as Y5. The preparation done by a primary school can prepare the child with ASC well and works best when it is in partnership with the secondary school. Secondary school transition has improved greatly over the past few years and many schools have good links and transition planning for all their new Year 7 children. However, there must be additional considerations for children with ASC.

Common issues

➤ The child with ASC may be vulnerable to believing or misunderstanding everything their peers and older children say about secondary school. They can be very literal in their understanding and so things like tales of flushing heads in toilets can be believed absolutely.

➤ Primary teachers may not know much about secondary school and may be over-anxious on the child's behalf.

➤ Parents may be very anxious, especially if they have not been inside a secondary school since they were children. They will be aware of (and may be focused on) negative or potentially problem-causing issues such as teasing, bullying, different teachers, homework, travelling to and from school and detentions.

➤ The child may have been used to having one teaching assistant (TA) for some or all of the school day. They may have had the same TA for many years. This can lead to an over-reliance on adult help or, conversely, they may have a strong desire to break free of an adult shadowing them all the time.

The secondary school usually becomes involved with a child's transition once the child has been allocated a place, or before if they wish to pick up children who have an Education, Health and Care (EHC) Plan. If the child has an EHC Plan, this will be passed onto the SENCO. Many schools have good transition plans in place that include support for all new children, such as interactive websites, transition booklets, taster days and even summer schools, and this support can be added to for children with ASC.

For the Year 6 teacher, preparation for secondary school can start at the beginning of the child's final year of primary school. If they are transitioning to a mainstream secondary school, it will be essential for them to use certain skills, including organisational skills. As many neurotypical children are also anxious about moving to secondary school, lots of these skills can be learned and practised by the whole class.

Staff can introduce the following support in Year 6 to help prepare a child with ASC for secondary school:

➤ Introduce a whole-week **timetable** so children can learn to read it accurately and organise themselves so they are in the right place at the right time. Providing opportunities to work in different parts of the school and with different staff for some lessons can help.

➤ Help children **organise** their equipment and books. Colour-coding their timetable with the colour of the subject books can help enable a child to get the books they need for a lesson independently. If their own drawer becomes too messy, put their books in a box near their table if possible so they have them all in one place, just like they would have their books in their bag at secondary school.

➤ Giving children **responsibility** (such as jobs to do in class and around school, e.g. sending them around school with messages and making them 'playground buddies' for younger children) can help them build confidence in interacting with a wider variety of people.

➤ Teach children **conversation** skills and roleplay how to introduce themselves to new peers (not too formally!). Teaching strategies for dealing with teasing and joking can be very helpful too in helping children with ASC cope with the many new children (of different ages) who they will meet at secondary school.

➤ Give children a year **timeline** or calendar to help them see the time between different events, concerning Year 6 and whole-school activities as well as those related to their secondary school transition. Add dates for when they receive their place confirmation, secondary school visits and taster days. Some children begin to worry about SATs, residential visits and the move to secondary school all at once, so to actually see (rather than being told verbally and having to remember this) that there are usual routines and breaks between these things can help calm them.

➤ Support children in doing their **homework**. Use a social story to explain why homework has to be done and sit with the child (and parents if necessary) to make a plan to help the child get homework done. Support strategies can include a school homework club, one-to-one help from a TA (at first), a home schedule or emailing homework to parents. Make sure that this support is structured and the child knows what help is available and what they are expected to do for themselves, that there is a time limit they can keep to and that their parents will check what they have done. Build praise and rewards (such as the school token system) into the plan.

Once a child with ASC has received confirmation of their secondary school place, a meeting should be called which the secondary school SENCO or Year 7 mentor may attend. This should begin with them meeting the child with ASC, and lead to the primary school, secondary school and parents making a transition plan with the child. It may be helpful to put a booklet about the secondary school together with the child and arrange extra visits.

The child may need several extra visits to the secondary school at different times of day, such as when the school is quiet and children are in lessons; a visit to see the dining hall, lunchtime and a lunchtime club they might be interested in; and a visit to find the location of the toilets, lockers and support rooms. You may like to give the child a camera to take photos and/or videos of key places in their new school (such as the toilets, reception, learning support room, changing rooms, dinner hall). They can put these in a folder or on a PowerPoint presentation to look at during the summer break.

Develop or make adjustments to the secondary school's transition handbook for children with ASC. Include a section on *What to do if …* to address their main worries and concerns. If possible, get a copy of the homework diary and a sample timetable from the secondary school. Tell parents how to colour-code the timetable with the colour of the books for each lesson. Advise parents on setting up a suitable space and routine to do homework, with a time limit and breaks, and teach them how to check what the child has done without doing it for them if necessary.

Transitions work best when the child and their parents feel well-informed, confident and reassured about this major change. The secondary school should take the lead in establishing good communication with the child and their parents and should ideally give them instant access to the SEND department to discuss any queries and issues before they escalate. It is the primary school's responsibility to hand over the right paperwork, share the strategies that have worked for the child and then support parents with clear information. They can then concentrate on including and celebrating all the child's achievements in their primary years and making sure that the changes to routines and activities (such as leavers' celebrations) include the child so that they feel confident and acknowledged. Many children with ASC have overcome many challenges, had to learn things in different ways and made personal achievements throughout primary school that deserve to be acknowledged. The primary school's last gift to the child can be a celebration and affirmation of the child, providing whatever support and access arrangements are needed to enable them to join in end of term activities with their classmates.

If the primary school has a Leavers' Book, they should make sure that the child with ASC has a book full of happy memories, that other children fill in their positive recollections of the child and that teachers, welfare staff and other people who have worked with the child are able to write a message or have a photo with the child. Make sure the child can get their shirt signed if that's what everyone else is doing, and do whatever you can to help them feel included and special.

CHAPTER 12
Conclusion

Autism is a diverse and wide spectrum condition. As teachers and teaching staff begin to implement the SEND Code of Practice, there is the expectation that class teachers will be responsible for teaching children with SEND and all conditions that cause barriers to learning. This is not a new idea; primary teachers have always known that they are responsible for the learning of all the children in their class.

Autism Spectrum Condition (ASC) affects every child differently and nothing can replace a thorough knowledge of the child, their strengths, interests, personality, talents and difficulties. It is hoped that this book will provide class teachers and teaching support staff with an easy reference that will guide them through a child's school career. SENCOs can use it to guide the long-term support for the child and to monitor that their ASC needs are being met.

Starting with the classroom environment, we can give children with ASC a tidy and sensory calming classroom in which they will spend the majority of their school day. Simple visual and organisational strategies can be used to communicate a welcome and an order that can reduce the stress experienced by a child with ASC.

Communication difficulties can be a major barrier to learning and interacting with others, but verbal and social communication can be supported in a variety of ways through the Early Years to KS2. Visual communication is the main strategy used for most children with ASC and for good reason; it can help support a childs' processing skills, develop their understanding and enable a child to organise their routine and self-check a piece of work.

It is important to help children with ASC become able to understand communication, interact with others and develop flexible thinking, and provide strategies, structure and resources to enable children with ASC to access the curriculum, being mindful of the strengths and difficulties they might encounter in each subject.

Sensory processing differences and difficulties affect over 80% of children with ASC, and it is important to understand and identify some of the main difficulties a child with ASC may have in this area, and practical activities to help a child with ASC regulate their difficulties.

As primary school staff support a child with ASC through the Key Stages, they should support the child's independence and organisational skills so that they can learn important life skills that come more naturally to typically-developing children. Social Stories can be used to help with this. These stories are a positive way to explain the world to a child with ASC and can be invaluable when they are facing a difficult situation that they do not understand.

Almost all children in a primary school exhibit inappropriate behaviours at times, and this is no different for children with ASC. It is important to learn how to interpret inappropriate and challenging behaviours in order to understand how logical they are to the child with ASC and support them in finding a better way to get their needs met.

Children with ASC often wish to make friends and this book gives lots of advice and support strategies to help them build strong and mutual friendships. It supports their social interactions and ability to understand what is happening around them, whilst enabling them to understand that it is okay to be different.

Finally, transitions, from the small and everyday to the major transition of leaving primary school to go to secondary school, this book will provide teachers and parents an understanding of the challenges this will bring and lots of support ideas and resources that will contribute towards a smooth and happy transition for the child.

The child is at the centre of everything that is written in this book. They can be supported to understand that having ASC is okay, that they are unique and wonderful and that there will be help and support for them whenever they face a difficult situation. Over the primary years, the child with ASC can develop and overcome many challenges and when they, their parents, teaching staff and SENCO all work together, it is likely that the primary years can be very successful.

Case Study

Nathan (Y6 pupil) said to his class teacher as he left primary school: "I know I am autistic and that's okay, because I've learned that it's okay to be different and that I can learn the things I'm not sure about. Thank you for everything you've taught me here."

REFERENCES

Adkins J & Larkey S (2013). Practical mathematics for children with an autism spectrum disorder and other developmental delays. London. Jessica Kingsley Publishers.

Attwood T (1998). Asperger's syndrome. London. Jessica Kingsley Publishers.

Attwood T (2006). The complete guide to Asperger's syndrome. London. Jessica Kingsley Publishers.

Autism Education Trust (2016). Transition toolkit. www.autismeducationtrust.org.uk/resources/transition%20toolkit.aspx

Ayres A & Robbins J (1979). Sensory integration and the child. Los Angeles, California. Western Psychological Services.

Biel L & Peske N (2005). Raising a sensory smart child. New York. Penguin Books.

British Institute of Learning Difficulties (2016). Factsheet: Intensive Interaction. www.bild.org.uk/EasySiteWeb/GatewayLink.aspx?alId=4090

Brown S (2015). Autism spectrum disorder and de-escalation strategies. London. Jessica Kingsley Publishers.

Carroll J (2014). Book review: BILD code of practice for minimising the use of restrictive physical interventions: planning, developing and delivering training. In *Journal of Intellectual Disabilities*, 18 (4): 394–395.

Challenging Behaviour Foundation (2014). Early intervention for children with learning disabilities whose behaviours challenge. www.challengingbehaviour.org.uk/learning-disability-files/Briefing-Paper.pdf

Challenging Behaviour Foundation (2016). Statement on restrictive physical interventions with children. www.challengingbehaviour.org.uk/learning-disability-assets/statementonrestrictivephysicalinterventionswithchildren.pdf

Challenging Behaviour Foundation (2016). Positive Behaviour Support Planning: Part 3. www.challengingbehaviour.org.uk/learning-disability-files/03---Positive-Behaviour-Support-Planning-Part-3-web-2014.pdf

Clements J & Zarkowska E (2000). Behavioural concerns & autistic spectrum disorders. London. Jessica Kingsley Publishers.

Cumine V, Dunlop J & Stevenson G (2000). Autism in the early years. London. David Fulton.

Cumine V, Dunlop J & Stevenson G (2010). Asperger syndrome. London. Routledge.

Department of Health (2014). Positive and proactive Care: reducing the need for restrictive interventions. www.gov.uk/government/uploads/system/uploads/attachment_data/file/300293/JRA_DoH_Guidance_on_RP_web_accessible.pdf

Do 2 Learn (2016). Do2Learn: Educational Resources for Special Needs. www.do2learn.com/activities/SocialSkills/index.html

Diagnostic and Statistical Manual (DSM-V) (2013). 5th ed. Washington. American Psychological Association.

Dunn Buron K & Curtis M (2012). The incredible 5-point scale. Shawnee Mission, Kansas. AAPC Publishers.

Dunn Buron K (2016). The Incredible 5 Point Scale. www.5pointscale.com/other_projects_article_5-point_scale.htm

DynaVox Mayer-Johnson (2016). Boardmaker online [Software]. Available from www.boardmakeronline.com

Edleson S (2016). Physical Exercise and Autism. Retrievable from www.autism.com/treating_exercise

Ellis Weismer S, Lord C & Esler A (2010). Early language patterns of toddlers on the autism spectrum compared to toddlers with developmental delay. In *Journal of Autism and Developmental Disorders*, 40 (10): 1259–1273.

Emotion Works (2016). Welcome to Emotion Works. emotionworks.org.uk

The Floortime Center (2014). What is floortime? www.thefloortimecenter.com/what-is-floortime/

Frost L.A. & Bondy A.S. (1994) PECS: The Picture Exchange Communication System Training Manual: New Jersey: Pyramid Educational Consultants

Fuentes C, Mostofsky S & Bastian A (2009). Children with autism show specific handwriting impairments. In *Neurology*, 73 (19): 1532–1537.

Gammeltoft L & Nordenhof M (2007). Autism, play and social interaction. London. Jessica Kingsley Publishers.

Goodman G & Williams C (2007). Interventions for increasing the academic engagement of students with autism spectrum disorders in inclusive classrooms. In *TEACHING Exceptional Children*, 39 (6): 53–61.

Gould J & Ashton-Smith J (2011). Missed diagnosis or misdiagnosis? Girls and women on the autistic spectrum. In *Good Autism Practice (GAP)*, 12 (1): 34–41.

Grandin T & Panek R (2013). The autistic brain: thinking across the spectrum. New York. Houghton Mifflin.

Gray C & White A (2001). My Social Stories Book. London. Jessica Kingsley Publishers.

Gray C (2010). The new social story book. Arlington, Texas. Future Horizons.

Gray C (2015). It's NOT a social story if... A screening instrument. carolgraysocialstories.com/wp-content/uploads/2015/09/It-is-NOT-a-Social-Story-if....pdf

Hewett D & Firth G (2016). Intensive Interaction [DVD]. Available from www.intensiveinteraction.co.uk

HM Government UK (2014a). P scales: attainment targets for pupils with SEN. www.gov.uk/government/publications/p-scales-attainment-targets-for-pupils-with-sen

HM Government UK (2014b). SEND code of practice: 0 to 25 years. www.gov.uk/government/publications/send-code-of-practice-0-to-25

HM Government UK (2014c). SEND code of practice: 0 to 25 years. www.gov.uk/government/publications/send-code-of-practice-0-to-25

HM Government UK (2016). Standards and Testing Agency. www.gov.uk/government/organisations/standards-and-testing-agency

Hodgdon L (1995). Visual strategies for improving communication. Troy, Michigan. QuirkRoberts Publishers.

Johnston P & Hatton S (2003). Conversations in autism. Kidderminster. BILD Publications.

Johnston P & Hatton S (2016). Coping with change: an interview with Paula Johnston, an adult with autism. www.aettraininghubs.org.uk/wp-content/uploads/2012/05/28.1-Johnston-and-Hatton.pdf

Koomar J, Kranowitz C, Szklut S & Balzer-Martin L (2007). Answers to questions teachers ask about sensory integration: forms, checklists, and practical tools for teachers and parents. Texas. Future Horizons.

Kranowitz C (2005). The out-of-sync child. New York. Skylight Press / Perigee.

LeGoff D, Gomez De La Cuesta G, Krauss G & Baron-Cohen S (2014). LEGO-Based Therapy. London. Jessica Kingsley Publishers.

Makaton (2016). Resources available from www.makaton.org

Moor J (2008). Playing, laughing and learning with children on the autism spectrum. London. Jessica Kingsley Publishers.

Moyes R (2013). Addressing the challenging behaviour of children with high-functioning autism/Asperger syndrome in the classroom. London. Jessica Kingsley Publishers.

Narsaria R (2013). Autism and Asperger brains wired differently, EEG records support recent changes in DSM- 5. www.autismdailynewscast.com/autism-and-aspergers-brains-wired-differently-eeg-records-support-recent-changes-in-dsm-5/1862/dr-narsaria/

National Autistic Society (2016). Gender and autism. www.autism.org.uk/about/what-is/gender.aspx

NICE guidelines (2011) www.nice.org.uk/guidance/cg128/resources/autism-in-under-19s-recognition-referral-and-diagnosis-35109456621253

PDA Society (2016). About PDA. www.pdasociety.org.uk/what-is-PDA/about-pda

Rao S & Gagie B (2006). Learning through seeing and doing: visual supports for children with autism. In *TEACHING Exceptional Children*, 38 (6): 26–33.

Schroeder A (1996). Socially speaking. Cambridgeshire. LDA.

Schroeder A (2001). Time to talk. Cambridgeshire. LDA.

Sher B & Butler R (2009). Early intervention games. San Francisco, California. Jossey-Bass.

Steady A & Roberts R (2016). Moving on up. www.leics.gov.uk/autism_transitions_parents_pack.pdf

Steiner C (2003). Emotional literacy. Fawnskin, California. Personhood Press.

Sharples J, Webster R & Blatchford P (2014). Making best use of teaching assistants. educationendowmentfoundation.org.uk/uploads/pdf/TA_Guidance_Report_Interactive.pdf

TES (2016). Resources available from www.tes.com/teaching-resources

Twinkl Educational Publishing (2016). Resources available from www.twinkl.co.uk

Wertz S.R (2012). Improving Executive Function. Retrievable from www.autism-programs.com/articles-on-autism/improving-executive-function.htm

Whitaker P, Barratt P, Joy H, Potter M & Thomas G (1998). Children with autism and peer group support: using circles of friends. In *British Journal of Special Education*, 25: 60–64.

Widgit Software (2016). InPrint 3 [Software]. Available from www.widgit.com.

World Health Organisation. International Classification of Diseases and Related Health Problems (ICD-10) (1992). 10th ed. Geneva. World Health Organisation.

Yack E, Sutton S & Aquilla P (2002). Building bridges through sensory integration. Las Vegas, Nevada. Sensory Resources.

NOTES